HIGH-IMPACT
Marketing
ON A
LOW-IMPACT
Budget
101 Strategies to Turbo-Charge
Your Business Today!

JOHN KREMER AND **J. DANIEL McCOMAS**

PRIMA PUBLISHING

To my wife, Gail —John Kremer

To my loving and patient wife, Erin, and to Matt, Alan, and Jesse
—Dan McComas

And, from both of us, to all those who want to sell or
give away more of whatever they love

. . . .

©1997 by John Kremer and J. Daniel McComas

PRIMA PUBLISHING and colophon are registered trademarks of Prima Communications, Inc.

Library of Congress Cataloging-in-Publication Data
Kremer, John.
High-impact marketing on a low-impact budget : 101 strategies to turbo-charge your business today! / John Kremer.
    p.   cm.
    Includes index.
    ISBN 0-7615-0962-3
    1. Marketing I. McComas, J. Daniel II. Title
    HF5415.K6726   1997
658.8—dc21   97-18353
                                                 CIP

97 98 99 00 01 DD 10 9 8 7 6 5 4 3 2 1
Printed in the United States of America

How to Order
Single copies may be ordered from Prima Publishing, P.O. Box 1260BK, Rocklin, CA 95677; telephone (916) 632-4400. Quantity discounts are also available. On your letterhead, include information concerning the intended use of the books and the number of books you wish to purchase.

Visit us online at www.primapublishing.com

Contents

Introduction

igh-Impact Marketing on a Low-Impact Budget is a collaboration between two authors, Dan McComas and John Kremer. In this book, we try to give you the best fruits of our experience. Our goal is to offer you something more than either of us alone could do. Dan, who developed the 9/18 Relationship Marketing System, has a strong background in training, copywriting, and direct marketing. As the author of *1001 Ways to Market Your Books*, John's strong suit is generating lots of ideas for promoting your product, service, organization, idea, or cause. When you use John's multitude of good ideas with Dan's 9/18 Relationship Marketing System, you will create incredible marketing impact at a very low cost.

To make best use of our talents, we've organized the chapters of this book around our areas of expertise. John wrote the first chapter, "The Seven Secrets of Success," to provide you with a basic framework for marketing and publicizing anything. Whether you're advertising a product, promoting a service, building a business, or just living a good life, you're bound to succeed if you apply these principles.

Dan wrote the second chapter, "Sixteen High-Impact Success Strategies," to provide you with the framework for the day-to-day marketing of your business. The key to these success strategies is Dan's 9/18 Relationship Marketing System, which focuses on repeated contacts with prime prospects and customers. Dan's examples of copywriting, marketing plans, direct-marketing tips, testimonial solicitations, and surveys will help you develop and follow through with a consistent promotional program.

The last three chapters cover three areas: publicity, online marketing, and other promotions. These chapters feature an outpouring of John's tips, including ways to get free publicity in the media, marketing on the Internet, and a collection of high-impact, low-cost marketing strategies. Once you read these tips, you will be brimming with ideas and motivated to take action.

We wish you the best of success!

The Seven Secrets of Success

I can give you a six-word formula for success: "Think things through—
then follow through."

—Edward Rickenbacker

In marketing any product, service, idea, or cause, you have to follow some basic principles. The following seven principles are not really secret; they only seem that way because so many beginning (as well as established) businesses ignore them. Don't ignore them. Instead, write them down on a 3 × 5 card and post them above your desk or on your bathroom mirror so you are reminded of them daily. Then follow them. To make it easy for you to remember the seven secrets, I've labeled them all with a one-word summary—all beginning with the letter "p."

Secret 1: Planning

Developing a plan is the first step in marketing any product or service. A plan allows you to establish a basic road map for your success. Follow it, and you will get to your destination. For any new business or product, here are a few questions you need to answer:

What are you planning to sell or promote?

Who will buy it or use it? Why?

How do you plan to package it?

What will you charge for it?

How much will it cost you to produce it?

How will you create a desire for it? ← *literally articulate the pain/problem you solving*

How will you let people know about it?

In answering these questions, you develop a plan. Be sure that your plan lays out the step-by-step procedure you intend to follow to create and promote your product or service. Above all, be sure to allow yourself enough time. If there is one mistake that most beginners make, it is not budgeting enough time for each step. When they should be getting out publicity to national magazines, they are still stuck finishing the prototype for the product. Nothing can kill a marketing plan more quickly than being late.

In book publishing, major publishers allow one year from the time they get a finished manuscript from an author to the time the book is actually published. Why? Because there are still many steps that have to be checked off, including editing, design, copyediting, indexing, typesetting, printing, binding, and distribution. Moreover, many marketing steps require a long lead time. Book

Nothing can kill a marketing plan more quickly than being late.

clubs, for example, require at least a six-month advance notice before they can select a title for their club members. Most selections for the major clubs, such as Book-of-the-Month Club and Literary Guild, are made a year in advance.

Similarly, most national monthly magazines work at least six months in advance. If you want to be featured in their winter holiday issues, you must contact them by July at the latest—but you increase your chances tenfold if you contact them in May. And if you want your product featured in one of the large holiday catalogs, you need to send out information as early as February. Most of the catalogs have made their merchandising decisions by May. Few would be able to add a product to the holiday catalog after that date.

Your marketing plan won't always require such a long lead time. It's quite possible to work on much shorter notice. Local newspapers and magazines, for example, don't require such advance notice. Local promotions can usually be done with only a few months' planning. You can also do national test marketing with a much shorter lead time, especially if you use direct mail, classified ads, or targeted publicity via newspapers.

Never assume that publicity is free.

Secret 2: Publicity

If you want to create the greatest impact at the lowest cost, there is no better way to do that than by working hard to get publicity. Never assume that publicity is free. It is not. While it usually costs less than advertising, it

Celebrity Endorsers

The effect of an endorsement by Oprah Winfrey or Rosie O'Donnell is well known. But don't overlook other possible endorsements:

- Several years ago, Cabbage Patch dolls hit it big after appearing with Jane Pauley on the Today show.

- Spin Pops got a big boost after Jackie O bought one for her granddaughter Rose Schlossberg at Serendipity in New York City. Of course, it helped that the people page of the New York Daily News featured a story about the incident.

- Besides the sales jump that Tickle Me Elmo got from Rosie O'Donnell, it got an additional boost when it sat in the lap of Bryant Gumbel, co-host of the Today show, throughout an entire show.

- When a nationally syndicated column mentioned that Arnold Schwarzenegger's choice of water gun was a RoboBlaster, sales for that specific brand out-paced all other brands by a wide margin.

- When consumer awareness of its Depo-Provera contraceptive injection fell during the debate over President Clinton's health care reform plan, Upjohn Co. hired Maureen McCormick (Marcia Brady on The Brady Bunch) as a spokesperson for a nationwide Birth Control Matters program. Maureen was so effective that media began referring to her as a woman's health advocate rather than as Marcia Brady. More important to Upjohn, awareness of the Depo-Provera product more than doubled during the PR campaign.

usually requires a far greater time commitment. It is said that in retail there are three rules for success: Location, location, location. Similarly, in publicity there are three rules for success: Follow-up, follow-up, follow-up. If you are not willing to commit a lot of time to following up your news release mailings, you will not get the publicity you want.

Why publicity? Because not only is publicity less expensive than advertising, but it is also more credible. The quickest way to build your company's name recognition and increase its credibility is to get publicity. People are much more likely to trust a news article than a paid advertisement on the same page. That's why when Oprah Winfrey selects a book for her monthly Oprah Book Club on her television talk show, more than half a million people go out and buy the book. No paid advertisements in the history of publishing have ever come close to generating that kind of cost-effective response. Never have, never will.

That's why one word from talk-show host Rosie O'Donnell could send thousands running to toy stores to buy Tickle Me Elmo and create such a demand for the toy that people were literally fighting in stores to get the last one. The manufacturer couldn't keep the toy in stock.

My company has one rule of advertising: Never advertise in any magazine until we've gotten some publicity in that publication. Once the magazine reviews one of our books or interviews one of our authors, we can then measure the response. Then it might make sense to advertise (although it makes far more sense to go for more publicity in that same magazine). The only reason you might want to advertise in a magazine is that you need to promote your product at a specific time of year and, since publicity is never guaranteed, you choose to place an ad.

For more tips on how to get publicity, see chapter 3, "Twenty-Eight Ways to Make the News."

Secret 3: Persistence

In publicity, there is a rule called the Rule of Seven (which is much like the 9/18 Relationship Marketing System we'll discuss later). It states that if you want your prospects to take action and buy your product or use your service, you need to connect with them at least seven times within an eighteen-month period. Most marketers will tell you that, on average, it takes anywhere from seven to fourteen impressions before someone is moved to take action. Those impressions might have been created by advertisements, publicity, interviews, a store display, or a recommendation from a friend. But, if you want to make the sale, those impressions have to be created. Once in a while you get lucky and make a sale the first time someone sees your product, but it is far more likely that it will take five, ten, or twenty impressions before someone is moved to buy.

Never think that because you place a full-page advertisement in *Popular Photography* for your new camera widget that you will have done everything you need to do to sell to everyone who could possibly want your widget. It would be nice if marketing worked that way, but it doesn't. My *1001 Ways to Market Your Books* is now in its fifth edition, has been publicized dozens of times in every publication for writers and publishers, has been displayed over and over again at major conventions, has been promoted in every speech I've given over the past ten years, and has incredible word-of-mouth—and yet it has only sold thirty thousand copies. After all these years, I still meet people who have been in the publishing business for

Once in a while you get lucky and make a sale the first time someone sees your product, but it is far more likely that it will take five, ten, or twenty impressions before someone is moved to buy.

Persistence Pays

The cornerstone of hot sauce cataloger Mo-Hotta Mo-Betta's catalog request campaign has always been publicity. They get that publicity, according to president Tim Eidson, primarily "by bugging food editors." The cataloger began by compiling a list of major food editors. They then sent samples of their Wasabi chips along with a catalog and a press release saying, "Try these chips; they're as unusual as our catalog." Every other month, the cataloger sends another sample, sometimes using an alternative delivery method such as UPS or express mail. Since beginning their PR campaign, sales have jumped to $2.5 million per year.

---

a long time who have not heard of it. Unbelievable! So, never think your job as a marketer is done. It has just begun, even after ten years.

 The smaller you are, the more patient you have to be, the more you need to persevere. I have seen more than one company close down just when it was on the verge of success. Several years ago, a self-publisher got a request for a review copy from an editor at *Ladies Home Journal*. The author mailed it out right away. When she followed up with a phone call several weeks later, she found that the editor had not received the book. So she sent another copy, this time via UPS. Again, the editor did not receive the book. In the end, she had to send five copies before the book reached the editor's hands.

Never assume, therefore, that just because you sent someone a sample copy, they got it. There are three known Bermuda Triangles in New York City alone—at least it seems that way given all the mail that goes undelivered in the city. There was a big semi filled with first-class mail sitting in the wilds of New Jersey for more than two years (a real case!). There was a postman in Chicago who buried all his third-class mail along with some first-class letters (another real case!). If you learn one rule of marketing in this book, make it this: Follow-up, follow-up, follow-up.

When he was promoting his book on Hollywood movie locations, William Gordon sent review copies and news releases to thirteen different editors and reporters at the *Los Angeles Times*. He tried every reporter he could think of, but none of them was interested—even though the book was about Los Angeles. Then one day, he decided to send a review copy to a reporter for the Orange County edition of the *Times*. Bingo! That reporter saw the story behind the book and wrote about it for the local edition. From there, the story was featured in all the other editions of that newspaper.

What if Gordon had given up with the thirteenth reporter? That's what most people do. Need proof? Read any magazine or newspaper in the world. Look at the stories it contains. Isn't your story better? Then why isn't your story in the magazine? The answer is simple: Someone else persisted longer than you. Someone else worked harder to get his or her story into the magazine. Someone else made that one additional phone call.

Someone will get a story into a particular magazine or get interviewed on a specific TV show. That is guaranteed. The media need stories, good stories. They need you. So who will it be? You or someone else? It is your choice. It is always your choice.

> **Read any magazine or newspaper in the world. Look at the stories it contains. Isn't your story better?**

Secret 4: Passion

I originally called this fourth point "product" because the quality of your product or service is an essential element in your marketing success. But as time went on I realized that it isn't quality that is so important. Most important is your *belief* in your product. That is what will sell your product or service. Without passion, your product is just another lumpy rag, indistinguishable from every other product on the market.

But oh what a difference passion makes! If you believe in your product, you don't hear a key buyer say no; instead, you hear her say that she needs more information. With passion, you take that one extra step. With passion, you create the best product that you possibly can.

I have one basic rule I follow when publishing books: I call it the Chill Factor. I won't publish a book unless I feel chills running up and down my spine as I write it. If I don't feel that kind of excitement for a book, I won't publish it. I won't even send out a news release unless I feel that same kind of chill from the news release.

Don't try to promote a product unless you have a passion for it. If you are going to do justice to your product or service, you need to believe in it. Why? First, because without passion, you will not persist when the going gets tough. But, second and more important, your lack of passion will show. It will leak out at the most inopportune times. Buyers, media, and consumers will all pick up on your passion or lack of passion. Don't think you can fake passion. You cannot.

Without passion, your product is just another lumpy rag, indistinguishable from every other product on the market.

If you truly believe in your product or service, you will not settle for second best. You will work hard to make it the best. Once you do that, the selling is easy.

Secret 5: People

This point covers a lot of bases, all having to do with marketing. First and foremost, your product or service must meet a need. No matter how wonderful its features, if it does not benefit people in some way, it will not sell. You should always figure out what needs a product fills before you take even one step to market that product. Then, whenever you are promoting your product, working on your catalog copy, or writing your news releases, you can concentrate on selling your product's *benefits* to people rather than merely cataloging its features.

A second aspect of people-focused marketing is customer service. *Always* give the best customer service. Don't just make a sale, create a customer. Satisfied customers are repeat buyers. And they are the bedrock for building any business. According to General Motors, a loyal customer is worth $400,000 to GM over a twenty-year period, both in direct sales and in referrals. Similarly, the average supermarket shopper is worth $3,779 in sales every year—if he or she is loyal to a particular store!

Remember: It costs five to ten times as much to acquire a new customer as it does to retain a current customer. According to Tom Peters, author of *In Search of Excellence*, it takes $10 worth of new business to replace $1 worth of old business. A study published in the Sep-

First and foremost, your product or service must meet a need.

tember 1990 issue of *Harvard Business Review* showed that if you could reduce your customer dropout rate by 5 percent, you could improve your profit by as much as 100 percent. What should these numbers mean to you? Just one thing: Treat your customers right. Make customer service part and parcel of your way of doing business—and make sure your employees do the same.

At Open Horizons, our guarantee says that all books are fully returnable within thirty days for any reason, no questions asked. In one case, a man returned a book within two weeks that looked like it had sustained three years of hard use (probably from copying every page). We couldn't restock the book because it was in such terrible condition, but the customer got his refund just the same. No questions asked.

Your people-focus should go beyond just giving good service. Also look for ways to attract people by putting them into your news releases and sales copy. How do you do that? Easy. The same way that journalists around the world do it: Quote someone. Read any newspaper story on page one and count how many times someone is quoted. Every good news story includes quotes from people. Your news releases should, too.

How do you get good quotes? If you have testimonials, use them. If not, invent your own quotes. I do it all the time. I'm one of the most quotable people around. For example, the news release for my book *Turntable Illusions* quotes me as saying, "Now anyone can experience the Fechner-Benham effect, the cockeyed illusion, the spiral aftereffect, the Benussi effect, anamorphic dominoes, and dozens of other mind-blowing illusions—all for one low

Your people-focus should go beyond just giving good service. Also look for ways to attract people by putting them into your news releases and sales copy. How do you do that? Easy.

price! And without using drugs!" That drug line worked wonders. Many magazines and newspapers, including *Playboy*, the *Chicago Sun-Times*, and the *Los Angeles Reader*, picked up on that line and used it.

On the cover of the fifth edition of *1001 Ways to Market Your Books*, I have a great testimonial from Mark Victor Hansen, co-author of the wildly bestselling *Chicken Soup for the Soul* series. It reads: "If you want to sell ten million books like we have, read and use this book." Now that's people-oriented, and it's also great sales copy.

Here's one more example of the power of a people-focus. Many years ago, a small publishing company known as The Little Blue Book Company used to test the titles of all its books. Some of its advertisements would feature one title, while other advertisements would feature an alternate title. In one case, they sold eleven thousand copies of *The Mystery of the Iron Mask*. But when they added a few little words to the title, the same book sold more than thirty thousand copies. What were those words? "Man," "in," and "the"—*The Mystery of the Man in the Iron Mask*. Which of those three short words do you think was responsible for tripling the sales of that book? Yes, you're right: "man." Again, the people-focus won out. It's simple: People like reading about other people.

People like reading about other people.

Secret 6: Positioning

No product should be given the go-ahead until you have a firm idea of how you will position it. That means you should always ask yourself the question: "Who will buy this product or service, and why?" The last part of that question is crucial. You should always be able to describe what needs and desires your product fulfills. David Ogilvy, author of *Confessions of an Advertising Man*, once listed thirty-two things he had learned during all his years as an advertising executive. Of all those items, he said the most important was how you positioned your product. Results, he claimed, were based not so much on how the ad copy was written as on how the product itself was positioned.

Personally, I like to hitch my wagon to a star. That is, I like to position my product by associating it with a best-seller, an already known product. For example, in promoting Nat Bodian's book *The Joy of Publishing* I began every promotional pitch by saying, "In the bestselling tradition of *The Joy of Cooking* and *The Joy of Sex*, now comes *The Joy of Publishing*." Since Bodian's book was about the history of publishing in the United States, the association with the other bestsellers made sense. The only sad thing, I discovered, is that more people are interested in food and sex than in publishing. A lot more.

In positioning your product or service, try to create a unique selling proposition, something that will set your product, service, or company apart from others. "We Try Harder" certainly sells the service provided by Avis. Here are a few other slogans that I think work well: "A diamond is forever." "Look, Mom, no cavities!" "Snap, crackle, pop!" "Don't leave home without it."

Each of these slogans is closely associated with a specific product. Note how well they sell the product. "A diamond is forever"—hence it's a perfect symbol of your love for another. "Look, Mom, no cavities!"—this slogan sold a lot of toothpaste. Of course now everyone wants whiter

In positioning your product or service, try to create a unique selling proposition, something that will set your product, service, or company apart from others.

Brand Names by Default

What's in a name? In Texas, KT&T Communications has trademarked the following names for its long-distance telephone service: "I don't know"; "I don't care"; "Whatever"; and "It doesn't matter." Whenever someone in Texas calls operator assistance and responds with one of the above phrases when asked which carrier he prefers, he is connected through KT&T Communications (which charges double what most carriers charge). I hope people don't get fooled more than once by this chicanery.

You can get business by default through such trickery, but if you really want business over the long term, you need to build brand-name recognition. That is the only way you can build true recognition for your company and its products.

---

teeth and fresher breath, so the slogan doesn't have the power it once had.

How do you want to position your product? Is it better than the competition? Cheaper? Faster? Easier? Decide what benefits your product or service offers, and then highlight the one or two benefits that make it stand out. Here, for example, is how Kiplinger sells its consumer finance books: "Kiplinger: Brand name help for generic problems." This is a great slogan. It says that their books can help you no matter what your problem—and that you can count on the help they offer!

Secret 7: Priorities

Remember that 80 percent of your business will come from 20 percent of your customers. Make sure you take

Remember that 80 percent of your business will come from 20 percent of your customers.

time to communicate regularly with those 20 percent (for help on that, see the 9/18 Relationship Marketing System described in chapter 2). In planning your marketing program, be sure to set your priorities right away. And then stick with them.

First, decide who your major audiences are. Who is your largest market? Your second largest? List your major markets, and then prioritize that list so your largest market gets the most attention. In marketing *1001 Ways to Market Your Books*, for example, my largest market has always been other book publishers. My second largest market was book authors. So I always spent most of my time marketing to these two main audiences. In the past year, however, something interesting has occurred. Now I'm getting most of my sales from authors. Publishers have, thus, become my second largest market.

How will this affect the way in which I write and market the new edition of *1001 Ways to Market Your Books*? I'll definitely add more material directed at authors. But will I change my marketing? Probably not. Why? Because most of the publishers who have bought previous editions will want and need to purchase the new edition. There have been so many changes in the past four years that all previous customers will need the information in the new edition. And those past publishing customers still far outnumber the authors who have bought the book this year. Nonetheless, I will do two things to target authors more aggressively. First, I will try to sell book publishers on the idea of buying copies for every one of their authors. Second, I will put a lot more effort into selling direct to authors by working with writers' associations, magazines for writers, and writers' workshops.

Think Big

When setting priorities, always focus on your largest markets first. Be realistic, but think big! For instance, Raven Maps & Images, a cartography catalog, has found it easier to get good publicity in national newspapers. As a result of an article in the <u>Wall Street Journal</u>, they received thousands of catalog requests and hundreds of orders. They repeated that success with several stories in <u>The New York Times</u>. But some of their attempts with smaller regional newspapers have gotten nowhere.

Remember to keep your focus on those media that have the greatest possibility of generating sales for you. Think big. Even the largest media need good stories—and need them day after day.

In setting priorities, don't just prioritize your markets or audiences. Also focus on how you are going to reach those markets. In marketing, you should be able to identify at least five specific audiences for your product. Then, once you've identified and prioritized those audiences, think of at least five ways to market to each of those audiences. Then prioritize those. When you are finished, you should have a 5 × 5 grid, or a total of twenty-five ways you could market your product or service. Then start with your largest market and the best way to reach that market—and go after it aggressively. Don't waste time on the lesser markets until you've done all you can to reach your largest markets.

Probably the greatest mistake that beginning marketers make is to scatter their efforts over too many markets. Don't make that mistake. Set your priorities, and then stick with them.

You should be able to identify at least five specific audiences for your product.

Secret 8: Plus

Always give them more than you promised—or more than they expected. At the beginning of this chapter, I promised you the *seven* secrets of success in marketing. Well, the truth is there are at least eight. And this one might be the most important of all. If you always deliver more than you promised, you will generate word-of-mouth publicity that will do more for your sales than any amount of advertising, publicity, or promotion.

In the past two years, for example, I've done no advertising or publicity for *1001 Ways to Market Your Books*—and yet I've sold more books this year than last year, and more books last year than the year before. Why? Because the book gets incredible word-of-mouth publicity. And that's because I've created a book that offers far more than 1,001 ways to market your book.

Surprise people: Give them more than you promised, and you will create customers who will come back to you again and again.

Secret 9: The Power of One

I've always had this problem: adding on one thing after another, always giving more than I promised. And here I go again. But this last point is so important, especially for those who want high-impact marketing on a low-impact budget. My point is simple: Ultimately there is only one person who has all the power to make your product or

---

If you always deliver more than you promised, you will generate word-of-mouth publicity that will do more for your sales than any amount of advertising, publicity, or promotion.

service a nationwide hit . . . or a local bust. That person is
you. You have the power. *Or the 1 person who*

It doesn't always have to be you. Sometimes you get
lucky and someone else loves your product or service so
much that they sell thousands or millions for you. For example, there is one bookseller in San Francisco who has
hand sold a thousand copies of one book that she loved so
much she told everyone about it. And there's another
woman who bought a copy of *50 Simple Ways to Save the
Earth* for everyone in her community—all thirty thousand
of them! And then, of course, there is Oprah Winfrey, who
can sell a million copies of a book simply by selecting it
for her Oprah Book Club on the Air—something she has
done consistently month after month since starting her
club in November 1996.

Here's one more example of the power of one lone
voice. In September 1984, William Morrow published an
exercise book called *Callanetics* by Callan Pinckney. After
the first round of publicity, the publisher sold about ten
thousand copies and reprinted another five thousand. But
then they ran into a snag. About the same time, Simon &
Schuster came out with another exercise book, this one
written by the actress Victoria Principal. In short order,
William Morrow gave up on Callan's book because Victoria was getting all the talk-show appearances. In time,
Callan also gave up on her book.

About a year later, though, Callan got a phone call
from a fan in Chicago who asked if Callan would be making an appearance in her city. Callan said she would be
able to come if she could do a television show in the area.

A half-hour later, the fan called back to tell Callan that she was booked on *A.M. Chicago*. Within hours of Callan's appearance on the show, Kroch's & Brentano's had taken more than four hundred orders for her book. That was in August 1985. From there, Callan went on to do other shows in Dayton, Indianapolis, Cleveland, and many other smaller cities. Each time she created another spurt of sales for her book. During this time she personally called the major bookstore chains to let them know that Morrow still had her books in print, stored in its New York warehouse. She had to fight with Morrow to get her books into the bookstores. But after about three months of persevering, her book finally hit the bestseller lists (over a year after the book was published!) and remained on the lists for almost a year. The book went on to sell 250,000 copies and garner a $200,000 advance for paperback rights. All because of one person.

Callan was lucky. One lonely fan in Chicago made all the difference in the world for her book. But her book could have become a bestseller much sooner if she had not given up on it so quickly. Callan could have been that one person. She could have taken responsibility for promoting her book right from the start. She could have made the phone calls. She could have confirmed the bookings. If she had, her book would have become a bestseller a year earlier.

The reality is that no one else can love your product or service as much as you can. Ultimately there is only one person who is responsible for the success or failure of your product or service, and that person is you. And the

> Ultimately there is only one person who is responsible for the success or failure of your product or service, and that person is you.

amazing thing is that it doesn't take a huge time commitment for success to happen. All you have to do is follow this one rule: Do five promotions a day.

That's it. Do five promotions each and every day (with a day off every once in a while for good behavior). Make a phone call. Write a letter to an important editor. Send out a catalog to a key sales contact. Handwrite a little note on the news release you send to a targeted medium. Make a follow-up phone call. Do at least five promotions a day, and within a year you'll have made more than fifteen hundred prime contacts.

I guarantee that if you make five legitimate contacts each and every day for a year, you'll make sales. You can't generate that kind of activity and not get a response. As long as you are targeting your promotions appropriately, you should create a tidal wave of response. But you have to be consistent. Do something every day.

To help you carry out those five promotions a day, the following chapters will describe a key high-impact, low-cost marketing program: the 9/18 Relationship Marketing System. Use this system as the foundation for your marketing plan, and you'll find that the seven—oops, nine—marketing secrets I've just outlined will be a snap to achieve.

The reality is that no one else can love your product or service as much as you can.

Sixteen High-Impact Success Strategies

2

Little happens in a relationship until the individuals learn to trust each other.
—David W. Johnson

The most successful companies and individuals are marketing driven. Your marketing efforts should have one objective: to open doors and shorten the selling cycle. Every day, you must focus on generating and re-selling customers. You do this by developing a systematic marketing process designed to reach the right people at the right time with the right marketing messages and of-fers. When you're marketing effectively, sales should be an easier, more natural conclusion to the process of get-ting your products or services into the hands of your buy-ers. If your goal is long-term profitability, you must focus on creating a relationship with your customers based on trust. Keep in mind that relationships are maintained by frequent contact.

Strategy 1: The 9/18 Relationship Marketing System

The 9/18 Relationship Marketing System is the conceptual foundation of this book. The tools, techniques, and strategies that follow are integral components you will use to launch and sustain your moneymaking process. This automated database marketing system relies on personal contacts and multiple mailings—a minimum of nine in eighteen months (hence the name of the system). Its primary purpose is to build rapport, empathy, and *lasting relationships* with your key audiences, suspects (those who have yet to identify themselves as prospective customers or clients), prospects, former customers, current customers, vendors, centers of influence (those who may not buy from you but who can refer business your way), and the media. With careful planning and commitment this system will dramatically increase awareness, acceptance, preference, and demand for your products and services. Here's how it works:

- ➡ **Establish and maintain a database** of your target audiences—prospects, customers, clients, media contacts, and suppliers.
- ➡ **Reflect an attitude of giving instead of getting.** Every other month over the next eighteen months, communicate useful information de-

signed to educate, motivate, benefit, or reward your target audiences in exchange for responding to you.

✓➤ **Follow up your contacts.** The mailing campaign can and often should be interspersed with personal telephone calls and face-to-face meetings.

➤ **Build a relationship.** As their confidence and trust in you grows, watch your leads, sales, repeat sales, media exposure, and profits soar!

➤ **Repeat the cycle** with your prime prospects and current customers.

Eighty percent of success is just showing up.
—Woody Allen

When people have choices, they invariably go where they are made to feel special, important, and appreciated. The most effective strategy for leveraging your marketing efforts is to consistently communicate customer-centered information and advice that builds trust and confidence in you, your company, and your products or services. The 9/18 Relationship Marketing System will help you reach this goal efficiently and economically.

One of the costliest marketing and selling mistakes you can make is to ask for the order before you know your prospects' wants and needs. This ill-fated strategy, says Steven Covey, author of *The 7 Habits of Highly Effective People*, is "attempting to make a withdrawal before you've made any deposits."

The most effective strategy for leveraging your marketing efforts is to consistently communicate customer-centered information and advice that builds trust and confidence in you, your company, and your products or services.

Picture this: You've just made a sales cold call and somehow manage to get past the gatekeeper administrative assistant. You shuffle into your prospect's office and there staring you down is an irritated-looking prospect. You introduce yourself and your company, but before you can say another word he growls:

5 elements for your regular n/letter

> (1) I don't know who you are.
> (2) I don't know your company. — *personality + values – brand*
> (3) I don't know your company's product or service.
> (4) I don't know what your company stands for.
> (5) I don't know your company's customers.
> (6) I don't know your company's record.
> (7) I don't know your company's reputation.

Now what was it you wanted to sell me?

Ouch! The moral here is that the sale starts *long* before the salesperson calls. The above incident really sums up the crucial need for building relationships with your prospects, customers, clients, suppliers, media, and, in some cases, your competitors! For years McGraw-Hill has successfully used this long-term sales strategy to sell ad space in its business publications.

Consistent contact with your targeted groups maximizes your marketing effectiveness. Research shows that confidence and familiarity are primary factors in someone's decision to buy what you're selling—or to refer you to someone else. The other sales motivators, in order of importance, are quality, selection, service, and price (obviously, price moves up this scale if you've positioned yourself as a low-cost or discount provider).

Research shows that confidence and familiarity are primary factors in someone's decision to buy what you're selling—or to refer you to someone else.

Clockwork Communication Yields Profitable Results

Repetition works. Persistence pays. A study published in *New Equipment Digest* shows that 63 percent of the prospects who asked for information about a product took three months or longer to buy. And nearly 20 percent took over a year. Most sales fail simply because a marketer gives up too soon. In fact, several studies have shown that 80 percent of all sales close between the fifth and ninth contacts! Billionaire businessman H. Ross Perot has claimed that most people give up just when they're about to achieve success. They quit on the 1-yard line in the last minute of the game, a few feet from winning a touchdown.

In many cases, the last one seen is the first one called. The 9/18 Relationship Marketing System helps you create top-of-mind awareness so you'll be the undisputed provider of choice when your prospects are ready to buy and your customers are ready to buy again. Here's the good news for you: Most businesses will never approach their marketing in this organized and disciplined manner. One excuse you'll hear is that they're too busy to market. Yet when the work slows, you'll find them scrambling to fill the new business void.

Is this a familiar marketing malady in your business? If so, then make a commitment to communicate with your target audience at least nine times over the next eighteen months to keep your phones ringing, the orders and leads coming in, and ready-to-buy prospects and customers walking into your office or store. Yes, this system requires

A study published in New Equipment Digest shows that 63 percent of the prospects who asked for information about a product took three months or longer to buy. And nearly 20 percent took over a year.

patience and persistence, but it will yield profitable results when properly applied and sustained. You see, in
many cases a "no" now means "give me more time."
Thus, you must stay connected with your buyers and potential buyers through personal contacts and benefit-rich
marketing materials that get the right information into
the right hands, at the right time to make them say "yes!"

You're probably thinking: "I get so much 'junk mail,'
and so do my prospects and customers. Aren't my materials going to get trashed immediately?" The answer in the
majority of instances is a resounding NO! But you must
be vigilant about communicating information that offers
value, news, and helpful advice.

Why Do Companies Lose Customers?

The answer is simple: apathy. Companies ignore their
customers to death. You've probably read that it costs five
to ten times more to sell to a new customer than to an existing one. Here's another reason you need to routinely
stay in touch. Think for a moment about the lifetime
value of a customer. Your first sale may be $100, but over
time, with repeat purchases and especially through referrals, that customer could be worth thousands, even tens
of thousands of dollars to you. This system will help you
cement this critical bond. What's more, by communicating regularly, even when you come in second on a proposal or bid, you will be positioned for success when your
competitor falls from grace by making mistakes or becoming indifferent.

Think for a moment about the lifetime value of a customer. Your first sale may be $100, but over time, with repeat purchases and especially through referrals, that customer could be worth thousands, even tens of thousands of dollars to you.

Results-Driven Marketing
Tools and Techniques

The list that follows features many of the techniques that you can use to create an ongoing marketing communications system to build trust and generate more leads, sales, and repeat sales. Many of these tools and techniques are interactive, direct-response vehicles designed to open a dialog with your target audience and elicit a reply. Several of these methods will help you sell your products or services immediately, while others will take more time:

- Mail preheat letters to warm up prospects.
- Send lead-generating and sales-closing letters.
- Send out serial sales letters—a timed-sequence of three to twelve personal, nurturing letters to grow winning relationships.
- Use complete direct-mail packages.
- Telemarket to generate leads, set appointments, and close sales.
- Place classified and small space ads in select business or consumer publications.
- Write general articles of interest and mail them to your prospects and customers.
- Get your articles published in a newspaper, industry newsletter, or trade publication (article reprints are excellent sales tools).
- Join chambers, associations, and networking groups and attend (really attend!) the meetings.
- Send your news releases to the media and to your prospects and customers.

- Sponsor an open house mixer or mini-seminar at your office for your best clients and prospects.

- Offer a free seminar and create a news release to announce it. Remember to invite the media. Later, send a seminar highlights report to those who didn't attend and invite them to call you with any questions about the material you covered.

- Teach an adult education class and inform your target audience as well as the media via news releases.

- Mail a needs assessment survey for proactive customer relations or to survey prospects.

- Write case studies of problems you've solved or opportunities you've created for your clients and mail to your prospects and the media.

- Create print, audio, or video brochures, sell sheets, and fliers.

- Use Q&A formats to answer typical questions or objections your target audience consistently raises.

- Conduct a VIP or preferred-customer private sale.

- Place yellow pages ads.

- Run radio and television commercials.

- Test a television infomercial.

- Mail out postcards.

- Alert your customers to new products and services with post-purchase communications.

- Be remembered by giving your customers ad specialties or imprinted promotional products.

- Send thank-you cards and letters for customer purchases and referrals.

- Use a three-dimensional promotion.

> This list is only a beginning. Once you begin communicating regularly with your customers and prospects, you'll think of many other ways to keep in touch with them.

- ➥ Attend and exhibit at trade shows.
- ➥ Ask for referrals.
- ➥ Use endorsed referral letters.
- ➥ Get involved in your community.
- ➥ Piggyback inserts (mail offers with your invoices, or include your offer along with a strategic partner's mailing).
- ➥ Conduct cross promotions with others.
- ➥ Fax broadcast your message.
- ➥ Set up a fax-on-demand system with informative reports.
- ➥ Send out e-mail messages to prospects.
- ➥ Use an automated infobot to provide immediate feedback to prospects via the Internet.
- ➥ Set up and maintain an Internet Web site that targets your prime prospects and customers.
- ➥ Send seasonal greetings, birthday cards, and gifts.

This list is only a beginning. Once you begin communicating regularly with your customers and prospects, you'll think of many other ways to keep in touch with them. For the record, the 9/18 Relationship Marketing System helped me personally sell more than $1 million in business for a small ad agency in less than eighteen months and currently keeps prospective clients consistently calling me for business.

How long should you keep communicating with your prospects? Great question. It's ultimately up to you, but I have gotten clients to do business with me after one, five, even ten years of ongoing communication. The question is, "How seriously do you want to do business with them?"

Now it's your turn to tap into this money-making relationship-building system.

Strategy 2: Educate Your Customers

Knowledge is power . . . but it's also profits! Here's why educating your customers and prospects on the advantages you offer will give you a decided marketing edge.

Taking the Skeptics to Task

Buyers in today's marketplace have a mind-numbing array of choices and can find it difficult to differentiate with today's profusion of parity products and services. They are dubious. And they're often downright persnickety. You must also overcome people's natural inclination to be skeptical or apathetic toward your business. Education breaks down the wall of consumer resistance by building credibility and confidence in the minds of your readers, listeners, and viewers.

When you're marketing properly, you will never be guilty of bragging about yourself. Why? Because you'll benefit from your prospects' perception that you can help them solve a problem, increase productivity, decrease costs, save time, or find new solutions to old problems. The key to a successful customer education campaign is to communicate clearly and consistently plenty of useful information to help your target audience understand your problem-solving advantages.

Establish Yourself As an Authority

Marketing consultant Trey Ryder says that when you use education-based marketing, you don't need to sell in the traditional sense. Instead you identify the person's problem and the solutions you can provide during every step in the process. He says that credibility builds trust and eventually persuades people to work with or buy from you.

he Reasons Why

important reason to educate your prospects and Effective education-based marketing gives irresistible reasons why your product or ser- ior and indispensable in the lives of your cus- provides specific evidence of the emotional /ou're promising as well as the logical reasons The box on pages 32–33 is an example I wrote ve clients to explain why I love personal coach- sulting programs, and how these programs can ucceed faster.

3: Use Free Reports
t Prospects

/e strategy for generating qualified prospect leads is to offer a free special report or other useful infor- mation. Your classified ad, display ad, or postcard has al- ready piqued the interest of your readers enough for them

Why I Created This Breakthrough Program

ONE TRUE REWARD for me is helping people achieve their goals by getting them to a place they may never have discovered (or may have stumbled on later by painful trial and error) without my help. Taking people's lives and moving them ahead to where they enjoy more control over their destinies—that's the real kick for me! This system and nationwide telephone coaching allows me to help a lot more people than I could otherwise.

Don't get me wrong. I do make money with my marketing programs. And so should you with the products and services you sell. That's the way it should be.

I know if I can give you the knowledge and tools to help you make more money with your marketing you will get closer to where you want to be faster! And the more people I can help to get what they want, the more rewards will be returned to me. This is known as the universal law of reciprocity. And it really works!

One of my clients, a real estate settlement attorney, was struggling with his practice. He decided to buy three boxes of my book Marketing Boot Camp and give away copies in person to his mortgage broker and real estate clients and prospects with no strings attached.

He simply said, "This book has been valuable for me. I hope it helps you build your business." In a matter of just two months his billings increased 20 percent. The next month saw another 20 percent hike! Several delighted recipients told him they were astonished that anyone would care enough about them to do something like this. Yes, what goes out comes back multiplied. That goes for money, time, possessions, and almost anything else.

Another Important Reason

Like you, I want more balance between my business and family life.

Maybe I'm strange, but I'm burned out on business travel. So creating marketing systems and coaching clients over the phone (in sweats, I might add) keeps me out of the friendly skies and away from lonely motel rooms and lousy road service. Now I can attend most of my boys' football and basketball games. I know Matt and Alan really like it when I'm there, even if they don't always say so. When you're twelve and thirteen years old, that's not cool!

What's more, I can wrestle whenever I want with my explosive two-year-old, Jesse. One day "Mr. No" will figure out why he always gets the last body slam and pin! Of course, one day he'll really be able to pin me! Oh yes, my wife and best friend, Erin, loves having me around more, too (thank goodness!).

To gain and keep business, you'll need to maintain an ongoing educational exchange with your database of customers, prospects, and suppliers. Yes, it takes more time, effort, and patience, but special reports, seminars, newsletters, reasons-why sales letters, Q&A sheets, advertorial ads, and case studies are powerful and profitable tools that position you or your company as the leading authority in your field. And, remember, people buy from individuals and companies they know, like, and trust.

to call for more information about your product or service. Now you must show them why they need what you have. But don't forget that your leads expect to receive some valuable information—some meat 'n' taters—not merely a plug for your company.

This free special report tactic works equally well whether you're selling products or services directly through the mail or trying to make your phone ring to set up appointments. A lawn company could offer a special report on *7 Ways to Keep Your Lawn Greener This Summer*. An attorney looking

Hint You can also leverage special reports by making them available free on your Web site or by providing them to various media to run as short news stories.

for business clients might offer *5 Mistakes to Avoid When Hiring a Settlement Attorney*. Your educational message can be as short as ten numbered tips on one sheet of paper or as long as you like.

Below is an example of an inexpensive lead-generating classified ad to attract prospects and the follow-up free special report. The ad includes a toll-free number and recorded message to increase inquiries and reduce your prospects' phone fear of being "sold" by a salesperson. You can also use this format with your regular company number and a live salesperson. Then, after business hours, simply turn on your answering machine or voice mail.

FREE REPORT: Increase your marketing response dramatically by using promotional coupons. Call 1-800-555-1212 for recorded message 24 hours/day.

In most instances, you'll want to send a cover sales letter along with your special report (see the sample report below). If you do, be sure the sales letter hits your prospects' pain/gain emotions while also explaining how they can order your product, your services, or get in touch with you.

Notice the resource box at the end of the sample report on the following pages with its call to action.

Strategy 4: Stay on Track with Customer Surveys

To help fuel word-of-mouth referrals, you must consistently provide a product or service worth talking about.

Special Report: How to Dramatically Increase the Response to Your Direct-Marketing Campaigns by Using Coupons

EVER THOUGHT THAT coupons were only for groceries? Think again! In these money-conscious times, many consumers are turning to coupons for all kinds of services to help cut costs and make ends meet.

If you rely on direct marketing to get the word out about your products or services, you need all the tricks you can get—because 95 percent of all direct mail gets thrown in the trash, most of it without even being looked at.

So what do you do? Use a coupon! When people see coupons, the words <u>free</u>, <u>save</u>, and <u>money</u> start running through their minds and they automatically reach for the scissors to cut out your coupon. Before you design your coupon, however, remember that there's a strategy behind successful couponing.

Maintain Price Credibility

The most important thing to remember when you're considering a coupon campaign is to preserve your regular-price credibility. If a coupon goes out too often, the customer will never buy from you when the item is regularly priced because he knows that if he waits long enough another coupon will arrive in his mailbox.

Take pizza coupons, for instance. You get them every week and stuff them in a drawer somewhere, right? And when you want pizza, where do you go? To the one with the best coupon, of course. With so many coupons available, are you ever going to pay full price for pizza? No way! See, by putting out so many coupons, pizza places have completely destroyed their real-price credibility.

To make sure this doesn't happen to you, offer something that won't diminish the value of your product. Consider a coupon for "Buy one, get one free," "Buy one, get a widget free," "Buy one, get 10 percent off your next purchase," and so on. Your offer still acts as an incentive to motivate the customer, but you're not conditioning the buyer to expect something lower than your regular price.

Looks Are Everything

You don't have to hire a professional designer, but you do have to make it look like a coupon. The best way to do this is to use a dotted line—something strongly associated with a coupon. You can also use a scissors graphic to reinforce the coupon motif.

Make It Clear

In order for your coupon to really pack a punch, you must clearly define your offer. Nobody will bother to save the coupon if they can't figure out what it's for! Make the savings, amount of discount, or deal obvious. Use color or large type.

Adding an expiration date also encourages customers to hurry. Experts suggest an expiration date no further out than three months, their logic being that anyone who hasn't used the coupon in ninety days is unlikely to ever do so.

Say It Again, Sam

Repeat information on the coupon that you don't want lost when it gets cut out (the name of your business, address, and telephone number). A coupon is useless when it can't be redeemed. You'll also want to repeat your offer on the coupon to reinforce its value in the customer's mind.

Prime-Time Location

If your coupon is part of a card deck, you don't have much say over where it appears. But do insist on exclusivity in the mailing—you don't want to be one of five carpet cleaning services advertising in the same pack.

If you distribute fliers or do individual mailings, position the coupon at the bottom of the page. If you run your coupon in a newsletter, magazine, or other publication and it doesn't take up the entire width of the page, place it in the bottom right-hand corner. These positions make it easier to cut out the coupon.

Test Your Advertising

Use your coupons to test advertising results from different mailers! That way you can see which campaigns are worth repeating. There are a couple of different ways to test your coupon's effectiveness. One is to print your coupons on a different color paper for each mailer you do. To see which coupon pulls better, simply count the number of each color that are redeemed.

Another way to track your response is to code each coupon. This is useful if you're advertising in a newsletter or publication where you have no control over paper color. Somewhere on the coupon, put a code that will let you know what publication the coupon came from. For instance, if you place a coupon in the September issue of the Local News, you could use "09LN" as a code.

For design ideas, look in the coupon section of the Sunday paper or monthly women's service magazines (such as Woman's Day and Family Circle). The companies advertising there are bigtime competitors, and they've got the art of couponing down to a science. Pattern your coupon design after theirs, use the ideas above, and watch your coupon campaign take off!

Hint Do you see an additional method to our marketing madness going on here? That's right! The document on page 38 is pulling double duty as a Customer Satisfaction Survey and a testimonial sheet! Smart leveraging, wouldn't you say?

Are your customers or clients thoroughly satisfied with the job you're doing for them? It's important to follow up to see how you're doing and make appropriate adjustments. Yes, it can be a scary experience and it can be painful to acknowledge flaws. But here's the good news: In addition to fueling word-of-mouth marketing, gauging your clients' satisfaction level will help you concentrate

Sample Customer Survey

Your quick response to the following questions will save you up to $50 on your next order of supplies!

Dear Valued EVCOR Customer,

To help us serve you better, would you please take a few minutes to complete the following customer satisfaction survey? To thank you for faxing it back to us by (October 5), we will be delighted to activate the enclosed Customer Appreciation Savings Certificate good for up to $50 off your next order of supplies. Don't worry if you've recently ordered; we've given you several months to redeem your savings.

Thanks again for your input. We look forward to helping you increase your mailing productivity.

1. Our response time on your service call was ____ poor ____ good ____ excellent.

2. Were you satisfied with our service response time? Please provide specific comments: _____

   _____

3. Was your equipment serviced properly? ____ Yes ____ No

   Please explain: _____

4. If parts were needed, did your technician arrive with the proper parts?

   ____ Yes ____ No

5. Are you dissatisfied with the current cost of your postage meter rental?

   ____ Yes ____ No

6. Does your postal equipment meet your needs based on your current mailing volume? ____ Yes ____ No

7. If you answered "No" to question 5 or 6, would you like to receive a free, no-obligation evaluation of your present postal costs as well as possible recommendations to facilitate faster, more efficient mailings? ____ Yes ____ No

8. Were you aware that EVCOR

    a. sells mail equipment? ____ Yes ____ No

    b. rents postage meters? ____ Yes ____ No

    c. provides free loaner equipment? ____ Yes ____ No

Fax to: 410-740-4121   Your Name _____

by (October 5) to activate your   Your Company _____

$50 Customer Appreciation   Address _____

Savings Certificate   City/State/Zip _____

      Your Phone _____ Fax _____

____ Fax or send me your complete list of supplies.

____ Please include me on your phone reference list.

____ We ship 50 or more packages via UPS, FedEx, Airborne, etc.

____ Checking this box and signing below approves us to use your remarks and name in our marketing pieces. If you do not sign, your name will not be used.

_____   _____

Signature   Date

EVCOR specializes in mail machines, postal meters, annual maintenance agreements, postal and shipping scales, postal counting systems, folders, inserters, bursters, decollators, letter/line openers, shredders, inkjet envelope printers, labelers, tabbers, and PC-based software systems for small parcel shipping. For questions or service call 410-740-0704.

on developing an ongoing and profitable relationship instead of a one-shot deal.

Above is a client survey format to help you generate ideas. Note how this company rewards its customers for a

$50 $50

EVCOR Customer Appreciation Savings Certificate!

This certificate is good for $50 maximum in savings on the following supplies when you fax your completed Customer Satisfaction Survey to EVCOR by (October 5): mail machine roll tape, fluorescent ink, pressure-sensitive postage labels, address labels, thermal labels, and ribbons.

Limit: One order per customer. This certificate is good through (February 19XX).

EVCOR specializes in mail machines, postal meters, annual maintenance agreements, postal and shipping scales, postal counting systems, folders, inserters, bursters, decollators, letter/line openers, shredders, inkjet envelope printers, labelers, tabbers, and PC-based software systems for small parcel shipping. To order call 410-740-0704 or fax 410-740-4121.

$50 $50

prompt response. Can you find an added advantage in this survey?

Now, let's not forget to reward our customers. Above is an approach to coupon copy you might include to say "thanks for your business" and to generate even more business!

Strategy 5: Your Marketing Plan

A person or a business without a plan is like a ship without a rudder: Whichever way the wind blows is the way you'll go. You'll end up somewhere, but it may not be where you want to go. To realistically reach the goals you've set, you need written strategic marketing action plan.

Marketing is a process and, as such, it never ends. Once the information is compiled and the plan designed, it has to be refined and revamped to accommodate changes in the marketplace. Here is a simple marketing plan format and calendar matrix you can use to create a cohesive, effective marketing strategy. Following the 9/18

Marketing Action Plan for Plants Alive!

Dan McComas

Speaker * Trainer * Seminar Leader

Marketing and Sales Strategist

11409 Catalina Terrace

Silver Spring, MD 20902

To: Jeff Kushner

From: Dan McComas

I enjoyed our meeting and felt it was very productive. I genuinely look forward to helping you quickly build your revenues.

Realizing you're on a limited marketing communications budget, here are the action steps I am recommending to get new business in the door as quickly and cost-effectively as possible. As we discussed, these recommendations are a starting point for our next conversation.

Marketing Action Steps

1. COMPUTERIZE. Crucial to the success of your marketing program is your database of prospects and clients. As noted in my book High Impact Marketing, you'll want to build a database of customer contact information so you can communicate with these people

on a regular basis. You're currently on the right track generating names via yellow pages and professional sources. You may also want to review Gale's Directory of Associations, available at the public library. It lists an association's meeting dates and locations 3–5 years in advance. If you ever need to rent a mailing list, my friend Brant Turner at Dunhill of Washington, DC, a list brokerage house (202-331-7724), can help.

2. DIRECT MAIL. Building relationships through the mail, over the phone, and in person is paramount to attracting new customers and increasing customer purchases. Over the course of the year you will send a series of letters, postcards, and newsletters to your various target audiences for special events, trade shows, and maintenance. I will write the first letter and edit the various follow-up letters you gave me at our last meeting. I'll also edit all letters and postcards throughout the year. Whether it's advertising or direct mail, you should always ask people how they heard of you and note that information on a new client form.

3. TELEMARKETING. Identify decision makers at the associations and businesses that are potential customers and for follow-up after letters are sent. One week after letters drop, call ten to twenty businesses per day with the twin goals of qualifying prospects and setting appointments. Post motivational slogans on the wall by the phone. You can get these kinds of posters at Successories in White Flint Mall.

4. SPECIAL EVENTS. Host an open house for clients, potential clients, and referrers. In your case, hold a summer barbecue with a tour of the facilities, volleyball, and other fun activities for your target audiences. Everyone should leave with a gift and, of course, information about new developments at Plants Alive! Also, frequently offer tickets, golf outings, and interesting articles to your clients and prospects.

5. ONGOING SALES, TELEMARKETING, AND PRESENTATION SKILLS COACHING. I will work with you and your staff individually and as a group on these disciplines throughout the year. Initially, I will monitor phone calls after the first letter drops in January and will offer suggestions and answer questions.

6. NEWSLETTER. Once a quarter, mail a one- to two-page newsletter to a select audience of clients, prospects, vendors, and referral sources. The newsletter should include how-to information, industry trends, referral contest (winners get concert tickets, dinner for two, etc.), new developments and products at Plants Alive!, case studies, testimonials, quizzes, and special offers or incentives for products and services.

7. TESTIMONIALS. Read the chapter in <u>High Impact Marketing</u> on how to get testi-monials and actively pursue five to ten past and current clients for their comments. Include these testimonials in future marketing documents. Also, obtain permission to use current testimonials in your promotional literature.

8. FREE PUBLICITY. Purchase and use the <u>United Way Media Fact Book</u> (202-488-2060), which lists all the television and radio stations, magazines, and newspapers in the Washing-ton, DC, area. It's about $10. You can also locate national media contacts in various media directories at the library. You must identify the editors at the trade publi-cations where you would like to be mentioned. Free publicity will help you build your customer base and provide important sales information for potential buyers. You'll also want to add a media component to your database and begin establishing relationships with the reporters who cover your industry.

Additionally, send a media expert letter (I'll supply copy) and Rolodex card to re-porters and editors. One of our goals is to get profile stories in the local papers and trade press to use as a direct-mail piece, a leave-behind document following a sales call, and to bind into your sales proposals. Let's also consider writing and publishing several articles for trade publications. Jeff and Dennis need black-and-white headshot photos. Les Henig in the Team Network will do this very affordably. Don't forget to read the trade publications for new business openings and new appointment announce-ments for appropriate follow-up.

9. FOCUS GROUP. Invite several clients and prospective clients to an informal breakfast or luncheon focus group to determine their level of satisfaction with your service and their needs and wants for the future. Participants should receive a gift for attending. If an onsite meeting is unlikely, we can conduct a client satisfaction telephone survey. I have a form for this.

10. ROLODEX CARD. Make sure the media, clients, prospects, and potential referrers have your Rolodex card.

11. ASSOCIATION MEMBERSHIPS. Join and actively participate in at least two trade groups where you can raise your visibility among prospective clients. For trade shows you'll probably want to consider joining the Greater Washington Society of Association Executives (GWSAE). We'll discuss additional possibilities at our next meeting.

12. ADVERTISING. Run small space ads in the trade publications read by your target audience. I'll also review and edit your yellow pages ad for maximum impact.

13. IMAGE ENGINEERING. You're making the right effort regarding truck lettering and uniforms. Keep up the good work. Also, give employees incentive rewards for referrals and ideas.

14. THANK YOUS. Remember to thank people—for buying, for a referral, for taking your call, for meeting with you, for giving you good service, for continuing to buy from you, and even for considering you but purchasing elsewhere.

Relationship Marketing System, this client doubled revenues after just one year!

On the following pages is a sample calendar for sequencing your marketing materials for one year. It is, of course, subject to change based on opportunities that develop over a year's time.

Strategy 6: Stress Your Product's Benefits

Understanding the difference between features and benefits is crucial to your success. Please pay very close attention. *Features* are about you and your product or service (what, exactly, it is). *Benefits*, on the other hand, are the specific results your product or service offers to your client or prospect (what, exactly, it does).

Just look at the marketing materials you receive. Most of them are selfish monologues instead of problem-solving dialogues. Or worse, they're just plain boring—the kiss of death in marketing.

Sample Marketing Calendar

	Special	Media	Trade Shows	Maintenance
January	Letter/flier/ Rolodex card/ price list/ testimonials Follow-up letter with qualifying calls and to set appointments Conduct focus group or client satisfaction telephone survey	Send news release re: Dennis as new associate	Letter/flier/ Rolodex card/ price list/ testimonials Follow-up letter with qualifying calls and to set appointments Conduct focus group or client satisfaction telephone survey	Sales postcard Obtain testimonials from satisfied clients
February	Newsletter	News release. re: 20th Anniversary Newsletter Send media expert letter	Newsletter	Newsletter
March	Sales postcard Telemarketing follow-up calls		Sales postcard Telemarketing follow-up calls	Sales postcard Telemarketing follow-up calls
April	Sales postcard Telemarketing follow-up calls	Write and submit how-to article to trade publication	Sales postcard Telemarketing follow-up calls	Sales postcard Telemarketing follow-up calls

Sample Marketing Calendar (continued)

	Special	Media	Trade Shows	Maintenance
May	Newsletter	Newsletter	Newsletter	Newsletter
	Invitation postcard for open house/ barbecue	Invitation postcard for open house/ barbecue	Invitation postcard for open house/ barbecue	Invitation postcard for open house/ barbecue
June	Host open house/barbecue	Host open house/barbecue	Host open house/barbecue	Host open house/barbecue
July	Sales postcard		Sales postcard	Sales postcard
	Telemarketing follow-up calls		Telemarketing follow-up calls	Telemarketing follow-up calls
August	Newsletter	Newsletter	Newsletter	Newsletter
September	Send either letter, postcard, or published article	Write or submit how-to article to trade publication	Send either letter, postcard, or published article	
	Telemarketing follow-up calls		Telemarketing follow-up calls	
October	Sales postcard		Sales postcard	Sales postcard
	Telemarketing follow-up calls		Telemarketing follow-up calls	Telemarketing follow-up calls
November	Newsletter	Newsletter	Newsletter	Newsletter
December	Season's greetings cards	Season's greetings cards	Season's greetings cards	Season's greetings cards
	Sweatshirt gifts	Sweatshirt gifts	Sweatshirt gifts	Sweatshirt gifts

Why do these documents inevitably fail? Because they don't immediately address the buyer's three primary self-interest questions: "So what?" "Who cares?" or "What's in it for me?" You see, people don't buy *things*, they buy *results* like happiness, making and saving money, saving time, popularity, wisdom, comfort, recognition, attractiveness, safety, security, and easier ways to do things. Technology may be changing our lifestyles, but our needs and wants have remained basically the same for millions of years. Be sure all of your marketing materials include payoff benefits that specifically communicate how you can help people to:

People don't buy things, they buy results like happiness, making and saving money, saving time, popularity, wisdom, comfort, recognition, attractiveness, safety, security, and easier ways to do things.

Make money	Love and be	Keep possessions
Save money	loved	Be entertained
Save time	Avoid effort	Become smarter
Ease the	Discover	Gain power,
workload	spiritual	status
Gain control	harmony	Exploit
Be popular	Be admired	opportunities
Be more	Gain praise and	Avoid mistakes
attractive	recognition	and criticisms
Be healthier	Avoid problems	Be more
Retain their	Make life	productive
youthfulness	easier	Make a better
Gain wisdom	Be safe and	life for our
Be comfortable	secure	children

Here's a case in point: An elderly man walked into a computer store and was approached by a salesperson who immediately launched into a mind-numbing monologue about the technological wizardry of a particular personal computer. The salesman was on a roll while his cornered prey listened patiently. About twenty minutes into the presentation, the man timidly asked if the computer would allow him to easily write letters to his grandchildren. That's all he really wanted to know! And that's the difference between features and benefits. The salesman failed to ask the right questions and went on and on about the features of the machine (what the computer could do) instead of uncovering and addressing the real benefits Grandpa was seeking (how the computer could help him communicate with his grandkids).

The Missing Links

Do you see the difference? Remember: Customer-oriented marketing always leads with benefits and follows with features. However, it's not always easy to be vigilant about communicating to the customer "What's in it for me?" To make this easier, connect the features and benefits of your product or service using words like

> You get . . .
> As a result . . .
> Which means you . . .
> This makes it possible to . . .
> This allows you to . . .
> So you can . . .
> Our new widget makes it possible for you to . . .
> We've been in business for more than twenty years
> > *so you can* feel comfortable and count on us to
> > be around to help you as long as you need us.
> We specialize in CPA marketing training, *which*
> > *means* we can define your problems faster and

recommend solutions with the likelihood of a favorable outcome.

Never assume people can translate your features into benefits. You must always do this for them!

Sell to People's Wants, Not Their Needs

We've all heard or read that the essence of marketing is to "find a need and fill it." Well, unless you have deep pockets or know exactly what the world needs, here's a fail-safe formula that will skyrocket your success: Find a *want* and fill it!

You see, most of us have enough food, shelter, clothing, and transportation. We don't *need* much more. But we *want* more. We need food but we *want* fast foods, diet foods, and gourmet meals. We probably don't need a six-bedroom, four-bath home, but we may *want* one. We don't need expensive designer clothes, but we *want* them. We probably need a car, but we *want* a Lexus or a Lincoln. We don't need sixty-minute audio tapes—we *want* to gain wisdom quickly and conveniently. We don't need insurance. We *want* security and protection. You get the picture.

Heart-to-Heart Marketing

Remember that people buy with their hearts first (emotion) and then rationalize their decision with their heads (logic). So, please, sell to people's wants (desires), not their needs (something required), and they'll reward you

Remember that people buy with their hearts first (emotion) and then ratio-nalize their decision with their heads (logic).

Tipping the Want Scales in Your Favor

People may want a product or service, but there are three problems that can hold them back from buying:

PROBLEM 1: Dormant Want—These suspects may have an unrecognized want but don't know about your company and your product and service solutions.

SOLUTION: Consistent education-based marketing makes people aware of your specific problem-solving capabilities.

PROBLEM 2: Passive Want—Your prospects may want what you have but are afraid or slow to make a decision, are evaluating your competition, or have an inaccurate belief or perception about your product or service.

SOLUTION: Provide an irresistible offer (for example, limited-time discount, 2-for-1 sale, frequent-buyer savings, iron-clad guarantee or warranty). Educate your prospect about your specific advantages including results-oriented success stories and third-party endorsements.

PROBLEM 3: Potential Want—They may want what you have but can't afford it now.

SOLUTION: Relax payment terms or offer credit. If they are qualified prospects, stay in touch (build a relationship) so they immediately think of you when they <u>are</u> ready to buy.

---

handsomely! How do you do this? By sincerely communicating payoff benefits and how your product or service can satisfy the three most important human emotions: hope, admiration, and fear.

Create the Payoff Picture in Their Minds

People don't buy for rational reasons; they buy for emotional rewards. Your marketing returns will take a quantum leap forward if you can help your prospects see themselves already using or enjoying your product or service. In other words, tap into their subconscious yearnings to create or feed a desire for what you are selling.

Pushing Emotional Buttons

In many cases your marketing message will have little to do with your specific product or service. Your goal is to help people *imagine* how your product or service will enhance their quality of life by painting vivid word pictures for them. For example, if you're marketing an enhanced presentation-skills workshop to professionals, make them see, hear, and feel the *experience* of receiving a standing ovation! If you're selling a boat, use a photograph or video to show it cutting through the waves with elated people onboard. A portrait photographer doesn't just create beautiful pictures—he or she preserves moments and everlasting *feelings* to love and treasure.

If you save people money, don't just tell them how much. Show them exactly what the extra savings will buy them. Perhaps it's their dream vacation home, a college education for their children, or a comfortable early retirement. People want to be rich, beautiful, happy, powerful, admired, and smart. They also want to avoid losing what they already have. Now, look at the list of payoff benefits in this book and help your consumer and business-to-business buyers see themselves already using and enjoying the rewards that your product or service brings to their lives.

Whether you sell to consumers or to businesspeople, you will always motivate people to action faster when you push their "pain and gain" hot buttons.

Vivid Words and Phrases to Awaken Desires

Gain

➡ Imagine having prospective clients calling <u>you</u> to do business!

➡ Picture your mailbox stuffed with more checks than you ever imagined possible!

➡ What would it feel like if you could _____?

➡ Have you ever dreamed of becoming a _____?

➡ Can you see yourself as a respected marketing consultant in your community?

➡ If you could paint a picture of your future, what would it look like ten years from now?

➡ Discover the fortune that lies hidden in your business.

➡ Now you can achieve your wildest dreams!

➡ Tired of just getting by? These ten financial rules will change your life forever!

➡ What are the secrets of looking your best every day?

➡ Can you really make sales while you sleep? You bet you can!

Pain

➡ You've read all of the self-help books yet you <u>still</u> feel something is missing.

➡ Imagine being broke in your "golden years" if Uncle Sam wipes out your retirement accounts.

➡ It was awful. Jimmy was up with the bases loaded and the video battery died . . . again.

➡ Are you paying too much for your life insurance?

➡ I was embarrassed to be the heaviest guy at my ten-year high school reunion.

➡ If I hit one more traffic jam, I'll explode!

➡ Could I have prevented these outrageously expensive cracks in my new deck?

➡ Do you hate wasting money on mediocre marketing methods?

Strategy 7: Positioning . . . Why Should I Do Business with You?

Do you know what the Marines want? A few good men and women, right? How about the Air Force? You're probably not sure. That's because the Marines have relentlessly utilized a simple yet potent marketing tool. And the Air Force hasn't. It's called *positioning*, and you can use this powerful concept to create consistent top-of-mind awareness with your prospective customers.

Positioning is not something you do to your product or service, but something you do in the *mind* of your prospect. How about 7-Up? It can't beat Pepsi or Coke in the cola wars, so it's positioned as the Uncola. How about Nyquil? It's the *nighttime* cold medicine. The "We're Number Two, but We Try Harder" position is a classic marketing victory in the battle for the mind and market share. And I'll bet you remember who said it. You see, in our media-numbed society, your message has to find a place in your prospect's already crammed cranium. So, the simpler your message, the better. What we're really talking about here is your *unique selling proposition* (USP). That is, what unique advantages you can offer that your competitors cannot. The good news for you is that most businesses have not articulated a memorable USP.

Now is your opportunity to define or redefine your unique selling proposition to distinguish your enterprise from the pack and give consumers a reason to patronize you. Once you decide, you must integrate your USP into all of your marketing materials. It's an exercise that requires cerebral sweat equity, but the payoff is being remembered at the crucial time when your prospect is ready to buy.

Caution: Be sure to communicate *specific* positioning examples. For instance, telling someone you're more convenient than others is not as persuasive as saying you offer evening and weekend hours, plus twenty-four-hour ordering and emergency service.

Why should I do business with *you* instead of your competitor?

Can you quickly answer this question? Your USP is the advantage that distinguishes your business from all your competitors. If you can't articulate your USP in sixty seconds or less, it's highly improbable that your customers and prospects will ever comprehend it.

Maybe you render more service than anybody else. Maybe your product has more quality than anybody else's. Maybe you offer greater value than anyone else. Maybe your discounts are greater because your markups are lower, or you give a stronger guarantee than your competitors, or you offer twenty-four-hour on-call emergency service. Once you decide on your strongest unique selling proposition, you should integrate it into all aspects of your business—advertising, personal communications, stationery, business cards, letters, and so on. Your USP can be different for various services and might include:

Once you decide on your strongest unique selling proposition, you should integrate it into all aspects of your business.

Price	Service
Value	Responsiveness
Design	Powerful Guarantee
Uniqueness	or Warranty
Broad Selection	Performance
Reliability	Convenience

Now, what are the greatest values, benefits, or specific advantages you can communicate to your prospects and customers that will differentiate your product or service most successfully from those of your competitors?

- ❑ Do you save people time or money?
- ❑ Do you make people money?
- ❑ Do you offer a larger selection?
- ❑ Do you offer free installation?
- ❑ Are you more expensive, less expensive?
- ❑ Do you offer better, faster service—same-day shipping, for example?
- ❑ Do you guarantee the lowest price?
- ❑ Do you offer a better guarantee?
- ❑ Do you possess technology that allows you to respond faster to your customers' needs?
- ❑ Are you more convenient: weekend hours, evening hours, 24-hour ordering?
- ❑ Do you give more than everyone else? For example, 2-for-1 or 3-for-2 specials?

Below are several successful USP examples you probably know well. Use them to jump-start your thinking:

Clairol makes you look younger.
Paine-Webber makes you richer.
Mercedes means safety and status.
Volvo is durable.
Budget Motel is economical.
Domino's pizza is hot, fast, and guaranteed delivery.

Allstate inspires trust.

7-Eleven offers time-saving convenience.

Hallmark sends love.

Let's say you're a psychologist. You could position yourself as the expert in female mental health. Even though most psychology patients are women, you're the one who says it!

To effectively expand your market, you can create an additional positioning name for your company. All you have to do is create a new division that speaks directly to your target audience. Let's say you're a financial planner doing business as Sally R. Smith & Associates and you've set your sights on getting more dental clients. Simply create and name a division called Dental Practitioners Financial Services and print up a new letterhead. That way, you'll be instantly recognized as a company that understands and serves the unique financial challenges and opportunities faced by dental professionals. Do you see how positioning is not as much about your product or service as it is about specific benefits delivered?

Save People Time and You'll Make More Money

With so many working couples, discretionary time is almost nonexistent. Anything you can do to save people time will be rewarded. For instance, QVC, a home-shopping television network, invites you to buy products from the convenience of your home. Of course, fast-food establishments are big business, but now Take-Out Taxi will pick

With so many working couples, discretionary time is almost nonexistent. Anything you can do to save people time will be rewarded.

up and deliver your carry-out order from restaurants that do not offer delivery. A telephone company lets you pay your bills by phone using a light pen, while a major food chain lets you order your groceries via an 800 number and delivers them to you. Meanwhile, shuttle-bus transportation companies are springing up all over the country to transport Johnny and Mary to trumpet lessons and soccer practice.

What's Your Promotable Edge?

What do your products or services do better, faster, or cheaper than anyone else's? Get busy and start writing down and communicating your unique advantages.

List three specific reasons your best customers would do business with you.

1. _____

_____

_____

2. _____

_____

_____

3. _____

_____

_____

Strategy 8: Irresistible Offers Lead to Faster Sales

Master marketers motivate people to take action in their best interest . . . NOW!

—Jeffrey Lant

That sage advice offered by Dr. Jeffrey Lant, one of today's leading authors and marketing practitioners, sums up the essence of effective marketing. Your mission is to get your prospects or clients to act on your offer sooner rather than later. That means using interactive marketing techniques that ask them to write, call, request free literature, take advantage of a free initial consultation or seminar program, return a coupon, or send a check. Remember, your prospects need (and like) to be given clear, precise directions—and it's your job to tell them what to do!

People don't like to change or to try new products and ideas. If you're convinced that your product or service can help them (and you'd better have that conviction or your sales will suffer), it's to your advantage *and* to the benefit of your prospects to motivate them to try your offering right now! Unfortunately, people are slow to move. Most will not respond to your first offerings. It's up to you to tell your prospects, clients, and customers what you want them to do and to make it easy for them to do it.

It's up to you to tell your prospects, clients, and customers what you want them to do and to make it easy for them to do it.

Rewards Make People Act Faster

A publisher offered university professors a choice between an attractive pen and an abacus as an incentive if they would read several chapters of an innovative computer textbook, provide their comments in writing, and return a survey card by a particular date. The promotion worked like a dream. It prodded the professors to open the book, read the chapters, and consider a new way of presenting introductory computer curricula. Additionally, thousands of cards were returned and the publisher's salespeople, armed with each professor's favorable comments or concerns, were able to gauge their prospects' degree of interest and answer objections faster.

Your Offers Must Be Relevant

Try to create offers and premiums that logically tie in to your product or service. Can you see how the pen and abacus mentioned above were appropriate premiums for professors in the textbook market? Such offers and premiums are only limited by your imagination. Here are several examples to stimulate your thinking and rocket your response rate:

- Offer free consultations, examinations, seminars, estimates, demonstrations, catalogs, samples, gifts, and survey reports.
- Ask for action—write, call, request free literature.
- Provide a money-back guarantee.
- Announce limited quantities.

➡ Use "bill me later" statements. (However, give them something extra if they pay with cash now. *Success* magazine gives away a free motivational book when you pay with cash to renew your subscription.)

➡ Use early-bird discounts.

➡ Offer mystery gifts.

➡ Offer private sales or charter memberships.

➡ Promote limited-time offers.

➡ Offer a free special report, booklet, book, audio/videotape, or checklist (for example, *17 Ways to Boost Direct-Mail Response* or *Money-Saving Negotiating Tips for Meeting Planners*).

➡ Make one-time-only offers.

➡ Use referral gifts.

➡ Offer multiple gift premiums.

➡ Use sweepstakes and contests.

➡ Include a detached reply device.

➡ Use involvement devices like check boxes.

➡ Provide free shipping.

➡ Offer a bulk-purchase discount.

➡ Make a get-acquainted offer—three free widgets—and they can cancel after that.

➡ Use toll-free answer lines or hotlines.

> **People naturally respond better to deadline pressure (remember final exams?) and will act faster if they feel they're going to lose out on something.**

Why are offers so effective? Think about human nature. People naturally respond better to deadline pressure (remember final exams?) and will act faster if they feel they're going to lose out on something. So, whenever possible, try to create a sense of urgency with time-limited, product-limited, one-time-only offers and fast-response discounts to boost your chances for greater results.

Strategy 9: Creating Your Marketing Materials

Before you create your marketing materials, you must ask yourself nineteen crucial questions. It's counterproductive (and costly) to begin writing your ads, fliers, sales letters, brochures, catalogs, and other marketing materials until you know your exact target audience and the precise advantages your product or service can offer them. What's more, if you're ever on a tight deadline, the following Q&A process can prevent anxiety and help you work smarter and faster under tight deadlines. It's crucial that you answer these questions—in writing—before you begin to write your marketing material.

1. Whom are you trying to reach?

2. What is the competitive situation? Who are your competitors? Why?

3. What do you want your marketing to do?
   ( ) to generate inquiries
   ( ) to answer inquiries
   ( ) to generate sales
   ( ) to build awareness
   ( ) to provide information
   ( ) to build company image
   ( ) to announce new products or services
   ( ) other: _____

What's more, if you're on a tight deadline, this Q&A process can prevent anxiety and help you work smarter and faster under tight deadlines.

4. What specific benefits are you offering them? How will it make or save them money? Save them time or work? Make their life easier, better?

5. What proof do you have to substantiate your benefits?

6. What will it do for them?

7. What specific problem(s) does it solve? What opportunities does it create?

8. Is your product or service unique or exclusive? What information or service will it give people that they can't get anywhere else? How and why is it new, better, different from what's already available? What makes people furious or frustrated about your competition's products or services?

9. Why should your prospects buy now?

10. What will happen if they don't buy now?

11. What obstacles are preventing them from buying?

12. What do you want the prospect to do?

13. How do you want them to do it?

14. What media are involved?

15. What is your budget?

16. What is the offer? Is there a special introductory savings? Premium? Limited-time offer? Two-for-one sale? Free information? Or, what will they lose if they don't act now?

17. Are testimonials or success stories available?

18. Do you have a guarantee (100 percent money-back anytime, thirty-day free trial, other)?

19. How will you measure the success of this marketing program?

Strategy 10: Write This Way to More Sales

When creating direct-response marketing documents— ads, sales letters, self-mailing brochures, and the like, use this time-proven formula to generate results. It's called AIDA (pronounced Ā-DA), an acronym for Attention, Interest, Desire, and Action—and it works!

Attention

Hit readers with an attention-getting headline to pull them into your document. Use your most important benefit or promise, offer, quote, question, challenge, news, value, or statistics. You've only got two to five seconds to grab them by the lapels and pull them into your message. Most readers never get past the headline, so you've got to answer these self-critical questions fast: So what? Who cares? What's in it for me?

Interest

Hit a nerve: Pose a problem your prospect is experiencing and then agitate the problem. Be specific about what readers will get or how your product or service will help them. Provide proof with endorsements, guarantees, or testimonials. Avoid generalities. Sell people the benefits or advantages your product or service offers.

Be specific about what readers will get or how your product or service will help them. Provide proof with endorsements, guarantees, or testimonials.

Desire

Get people emotionally involved. Make them say, "Yes, this is me." Let them see themselves already using, enjoying, and benefiting from your product or service. Touch on their deepest aspirations or anxieties. Get them beyond "I like it" to "I want it!"

Action

Ask for the order! Provide a specific reward or urgent reason to incite immediate action, such as limited-time offers or limited availability.

Winning Copywriting Tips

When you write marketing materials, you're not talking to a group of people. It's one-on-one communication. Check out the following strategies. Use them whenever possible.

➡ Make your writing sound personal, just like you're telling someone about your product or service face-to-face.

➡ Be sure you write in the language your audience understands.

➡ Use active words in the present tense.

➡ Be upbeat! Positive copy almost always outpulls negative copy.

➡ Use the word "you" and offer plenty of benefits. Examples: "you get," "you save," "you will receive," "you will accomplish."

➡ Readers are lazy. Make it easy for them to understand and respond. Write in a clear style an eighth-grader could grasp.

➡ In direct mail, try to entice your reader with tokens, check boxes, true-or-false quizzes, scratch-and-sniffs, and other devices to get them actively involved.

➡ Indent paragraphs.

➡ Use short paragraphs and short sentences. Like this.

➡ Include visual eye-catchers like boxes (❑), bullets (•), arrows (→), ALL CAPS, *italics*, <u>underlines</u>, **boldface**, or a second color.

Make your writing sound personal, just like you're telling someone about your product or service face-to-face.

P.S., I Love You

Always use a postscript in a sales letter because people *always* read it. Studies show that most readers will skim through a sales letter in this fashion before they devote time to read the entire document: They'll glance at the headline, the salutation, the signature (to see who it's from), and then go to the postscript. An effective P.S. can repeat your primary benefit or offer, introduce a surprise bonus, restate your iron-clad guarantee, or pull them back into the body copy of the letter with a statement like, "As I said on page there, this breakthrough software has incredible money-making potential."

An effective P.S. can repeat your primary benefit or offer, introduce a surprise bonus, restate your iron-clad guarantee, or pull readers back into the body copy of the letter.

How Long Should Your Copy Be?

As long as it takes to get your reader to act!

The typical objection to long copy is that "no one reads it." Listen. We've written four-, eight-, and sixteen-page sales letters that have been highly profitable. People will read long copy if they're interested in the subject. Consider this: If you were selling your product or service face-to-face with a prospect, would you stop after the first page of your presentation?

Think back to the last time you bought a new car or computer. If you're like us, you probably pored over every ad and read every brochure or specification sheet from cover to cover because you were hungry to learn more about it—and you wanted to logically justify your emotionally driven potential purchase. As a general guideline, short copy tends to be more effective for lead generation, while longer copy ("the more you tell the more you sell") is typically used for generating orders.

Hot-Button Headlines That Get Attention

Good headlines can boost your response by 100 percent to 500 percent! Note that 80 percent of readers never get past a marketing document's headline if it's poorly written. But this won't happen to you when you make a promise, offer a benefit, or present news that will give your audience what it wants. Statement headlines are typically stronger than question headlines.

Why? Because you don't want your reader to answer the headline with a "no," a "maybe," or an "I don't know." Question headlines can be effective, however, if you genuinely know the problems or wants of your target audience, or when posed as a curiosity headline like, "Why aren't all financial planners rich?"

Dan's introduction to marketing consultant Dr. Jeffrey Lant was through a postcard with a headline that read: *Hey Marketing and Sales Execs, If You're So Smart, How Come You're Not Making a Six-Figure+ Salary Right Now!* This challenge headline motivated Dan to immediately call Jeffrey and order two of his marketing books (and several more after that!).

In writing headlines, steer clear of clichés and cute or clever copy. It will only distract or confuse your reader. Your job is to get people to agree with you and to act!

In writing headlines, steer clear of clichés and cute or clever copy. It will only distract or confuse your reader.

Many copywriters read proven headlines for inspiration when trying to create new headlines. Use the following list of winners to help stimulate your thinking. Can you see what benefits or emotions each of these time-tested headlines instantly telegraphs?

Here's a Quick Way to Break Up a Cold

Take This 1-Minute Test—of an Amazing New
　　Kind of Shaving Cream

Imagine Me . . . Holding an Audience Spellbound
　　for 30 Minutes

Who Else Wants Lighter Cake—in Half the
　　Mixing Time?

Guaranteed to Go Through Ice, Mud, or Snow—
　　or We Pay the Tow!

Whose Fault When Children Disobey?

How a "Fool Stunt" Made Me a Star Salesman

Doctors Prove 2 out of 3 Women Can Have
　　More Beautiful Skin in 14 Days

When Doctors "Feel Rotten" This Is What
　　They Do

Do You Recognize the 7 Early Warning Signs
　　of High Blood Pressure?

How Investors Can Save 70% on Commissions
　　This Year

Play Guitar in 7 Days or Your Money Back

The italicized words below are proven headline attention-getters. Use them to boost the response of your letters and ads:

How to Win Friends and Influence People

Secrets of Successful Consultants

Warning: Poor Customer Service Is Hazardous to Your Bottom Line!

Are You Getting the Most Computer Power for Your Dollar?

10 Ways (Tips or Hints) to Save Money on Your Taxes

Introducing the Newest Energy-Saving Device from Myer Electronics

Announcing the Latest Breakthrough in Catalog Shopping

Attention: Video Producers in Need of More Sales

We *Guarantee* the New XYZ Fax Will Save You $75 a Month

What Could You Do with an Extra $25,000 to $100,000?

For Busy Salespeople *Only:* How to Make More Sales in Less Time

Now You Can Clean Windows Faster and Easier

7 *Advantages You Get* with Jenkins Auto Leasing

Who Needs Better Gas Mileage?

What You Should Know about Financial Planning

The *Easy Way* to a Healthier Lifestyle

Hint Author and marketing superstar Ted Nicholas notes that headlines containing quote marks draw 28 percent more attention. He says this happens because the words are perceived to be more important when someone appears to be quoted. Why not test your next direct response ad or sales letter headline with and without quote marks and see for yourself? "You Just May Be Our Next Direct-Mail Millionaire!"

Discover How Realtors Are Making More Sales with the "Breakthrough Farming" System

11 *Reasons Why* More Plumbers Are Now Turning to Smith Supply Company

Promising New Breakthrough in Mental Health Care

The Truth about Workaholics

"10 Marketing *Mistakes* You Can Avoid Right Now"

Magic Words That Pull Like Magnets

To get and keep your reader's or listener's attention and interest, work these motivating words into your marketing copy to trigger greater response:

Acclaimed	Extraordinary	New
Advancement	First Time Ever	Now
Amazing	Frustrating	Offer
Announcing	Free	Plus
Astonishing	Guaranteed	Power
At Last	How To	Practical
Attention	Hurry	Prevents
Bargain	Imagine	Profitable
Boosts	Important	Proven
Breakthrough	Improved	Quickly
Challenge	Incredible	Recommended
Choice	Instantly	Reliable
Compare	Introducing	Remarkable
Delivers	Last Chance	Results
Discount	Love	Revolutionary
Discover	Magic	Safety
Easy	Miracle	Sale
Effective	Money-Making	Save
Exceptional	Money-Saving	Secret

Sensational	Surefire	Wanted
Simplifies	Surprising	Warning
Special Offer	The Truth About	You
Startling	Trusted	Yours
Striking	Ultimate	
Suddenly	Valuable	

ATTENTION! We want YOU to use these TRUSTED, PROVEN, POWERFUL words to generate SURPRISING, yet REMARKABLE MONEY-MAKING RESULTS!

Guarantees Ease the Buying Jitters

The marketplace is jaded. Skepticism is rampant. Thanks to unscrupulous politicians, marketers, even members of the clergy, to name a few, most of us have joined the ranks of the burned buyers club. It's natural for your prospects to be wary of your offers and promises.

Tougher still, most people dread making decisions. They just don't like to change, and when they do, they change very slowly. That's why credibility is crucial. It's always incumbent upon you to show indisputable proof that your product or service will do what you say it will. One of the best ways to instill confidence is to include risk-reducers like:

Satisfaction guarantee	No-quibble return policies
Unconditional money-back guarantee	No-risk trial offers (send no money)
Price protection guarantee	Cancel at any time
Lifetime guarantee	Liberal return allowance
Full-year warranty	Your gift is tax-deductible

It's natural for your prospects to be wary of your offers and promises.

These strategies will help you overcome a prospect's reluctance to believe in you or buy from you. We guarantee it!

Strategy 11: How to Get Persuasive Testimonials

As much as people like to think of themselves as individuals, most folks harbor a herd mentality. When it comes to trying or buying something new, we like to know that others tried it and liked it first. One of the most effective ways to lend credibility to your marketing and quiet all those doubting Thomases is through third-party endorsements or testimonials. Unsolicited, customer-written testimonials are typically the best because they come from the heart. But we'll bet that you have many satisfied clients who have never written a testimonial letter to you because (a) you haven't asked them, (b) they don't have the time, or (c) they don't know how to write one.

As you'll see, the most effective testimonials focus on the benefits that you or your product or service have brought to the lives of others. Here are some of the results-oriented points that can be communicated in a testimonial:

Service/timeliness
Return on investment created
Responsiveness
Reliability
Special abilities

Quality
Accountability
Durability
Price
Efficiency

Unsolicited, customer-written testimonials are typically the best because they come from the heart.

Get a Powerful Testimonial
via Telephone—Fast

1. Call a satisfied customer (you do have one, don't you?). If you're a start-up business, ask someone whom you've benefited in a previous job or situation. Prospects are really buying you and your unique advantages. If you're selling a new product, use testimonials from your test or focus groups.

2. Tell the customer you're putting together your marketing materials and would like to include several comments from satisfied clients. Ask if this is OK. Virtually everyone will say yes!

3. Don't ask questions that can be answered with a simple "yes" or "no." Ask your client open-ended questions like: Please tell me how our product or service specifically helped you achieve your goals. What did you like most about our product? How has our product benefited you or your buyers? Until they get warmed up, most people will give you short, general comments. That's when you say, "Could you be more specific about that?" An excellent last question to ask is, "Are there any other ways you can think of where our product/service has been beneficial?" Don't be surprised if you only have to ask one question and your client gives you everything you need. People like to feel important and talk about themselves! They also like to be helpful.

4. Your clients will be presenting stream-of-consciousness comments, so you'll need to take copious notes. After the conversation, tell them that you'll edit their comments

for continuity and get back to them with a draft testimonial.

5. You'll probably have a page of comments to work with, which you should boil down to about two to four sentences. Phone, fax, or mail this draft back to your clients and ask them to initial it if OK or make any changes they like. In most cases they will immediately give you the green light and you'll have your testimonial.

6. Write out your testimonials in italic typeface (*like this*), or with quote marks (" ")—or both. Put your client's name, title, city, and state under the testimonial. Try to get a minimum of three. The more the better. Caution 1: Be sure you have an OK in writing. Caution 2: Vary your testimonials to address the results points previously mentioned. The more ways you can prove your problem-solving capabilities, the more new business you will generate.

7. Now, include your proof-positive testimonials in all of your ads, sales letters, brochures, news releases, and credentials kit.

Of course your testimonials don't have to come solely from your customers. You can also benefit from celebrity or public figure testimonials and endorsement letters; testimonials from technical experts or respected institutions and associations; editorial reviews, media quotes, reprints from newsletters and magazines; and the government. And don't worry about the effectiveness of testimonials diminishing over the years. Testimonials are timeless. It doesn't matter *when* you helped someone as much as *how*

Make Your Testimonials Specific and Results-Driven

ANEMIC: Your presentation was great!

STRONGER: In the three days since I attended your Call Reluctance seminar, my appointments are up 30% and I've already closed two substantial deals. Thanks for helping me to identify and overcome my personal sales challenges and for your empathy and expertise!

ANEMIC: Your news release really helped me generate a lot of media attention.

STRONGER: Wow! In just two weeks your news release generated worldwide calls and letters, a three-minute TV interview, and a full-page color newspaper spread. I literally received $5,000 of advertising for only $300!

you helped them. Of course, you'll want to update your testimonials as you gain more satisfying results for your current customers or clients.

Incidentally, calling customers for testimonials is a great way to reconnect with them and to generate repeat business.

Faxed Testimonial Request Sample

On the following pages is an easy-to-use letter/fax format you can use to get testimonials quickly! I used this letter to generate thirteen (out of fifteen faxed) awesome testimonials for my business in less than three days!

Now, take this model and start stockpiling tons of testimonials for your business!

Dan McComas

11409 Catalina Terrace * Silver Spring, MD 20902

Phone: 301-946-6636 * Fax: 301-946-6910

July 5, 1997

Dear Brent,

I need your help!!!

I'd like to get a testimonial from you to use in my promotional materials. Please feel free to use the form below to jot down your comments. Don't worry about writing structure. Stream of consciousness is OK—I'll convert your comments into a testimonial or letter format.

Would it be possible to fax or mail this back to me by July 22? Thank you for your help. And please call me with any pressing marketing questions or concerns you may have. I'll be happy to brainstorm with you off the clock. I also have a special report I will send to you titled 7 Ways to Powercharge Your Marketing as my way of saying thanks!

Best always,

Dan McComas

- -

Describe the one or two main benefits or successes you have received from my coaching, consulting, copywriting, and PR services that you value the most. Please be as specific as possible and tell me how these methods have improved your marketing, sales, and business life.

_____

_____

_____

_____

Thank you very much!!!

Signing below allows us to use your remarks and name in our promotional pieces. If you do not sign, your name will not be used.

_____   _____
Signature   Date

May I also include you on my telephone reference list? _____ Yes _____ No

Make a Case Out of Your Success Stories

People are fascinated by stories—especially tales of triumph. Your prospects also want to know about your track record or the results you've achieved for others. Case studies are highly effective tools to demonstrate your problem-solving abilities. They're easy to write if you follow the simple three-step Problem-Action-Results (PAR) formula.

Hint In addition to a grouping of short testimonials, you'll also want to include a mix of individual testimonials on your clients' letterheads. If they say they're too busy, offer to write it for them and let them edit the letter.

1. Problem. What was the problem your customer asked you to solve?

2. Action. What critical thinking, research, or specific steps did you undertake to solve the problem or to help your customer reach a desired goal?

3. Results. What were the specific outcomes? How did your

client benefit from the work that you did? What were his or her reactions to the good news?

You should include winning case studies or success stories in your ads, fliers, brochures, and proposals. Caution: Some success story details may be confidential, so be sure to clear the copy with your client.

Here is a letter that describes an incredible success story experienced by one reader of John's book, *1001 Ways to Market Your Books*.

Dear Mr. Kremer,

This letter is long overdue, but we haven't been able to stop fulfilling book orders (since we read <u>1001 Ways to Market Your Books</u>) long enough to write you.

When we published our first book, <u>Lifeline: The Action Guide for Adoption Search</u>, we had no clue how to get it into the hands of those who needed it.

A librarian recommended your book to me. I ran home with it and read it cover to cover in one night—making notes in the margins, highlighting key sentences, and jamming book marks into key chapters. Forty-eight hours later, I took my new knowledge to New York City to introduce our book at the American Booksellers Association convention.

Twenty-four hours after arriving and using your hottest tips and ideas, I had signed distribution agreements with Ingram and Baker & Taylor, sold subsidiary rights for software, sold foreign language rights, had three major publishers discussing mass market rights, booked two national talk shows, sold huge orders to B. Dalton and Waldenbooks, and still got home in time for dinner!

We have our second book in the works now and already your ideas have helped us get a six-figure offer from a movie company for the rights to the story!

Thank you! You have made our decade!!

Troy Dunn, publisher
Caradium Publishing

Strategy 12: Before You Invest, Test, Test, Test

How many medical doctors do you know who commit to surgery or a course of action without taking blood tests, X-rays, MRIs, and so on? Not many, we hope. We marketers are much like doctors in that we must know our target audience's pain and its hope for gain. Yet so many marketers fly blind without testing their appeals.

Testing your marketing minimizes business risk. And it can help you make educated decisions on your pricing, market, distribution channels, and more. The ultimate judge and jury of your marketing is the consumer. So you must always let the marketplace tell you what it wants—not what you think it wants.

> It's crucial to test your assumptions, your market, and your marketing messages before you roll out a large mailing or invest a bundle on an advertising or direct-mail campaign.

Marketing Is Not an Exact Science

Why is marketing not a science? Because humans simply aren't logical creatures. What people say they want and what they actually want can differ. That's why it's crucial to test your assumptions, your market, and your marketing messages before you roll out a large mailing or invest a bundle on an advertising or direct-mail campaign. It's much easier and faster to test if you're using direct-response marketing because you're asking people to call you, stop by, send in a response card, or connect with you via telephone.

Let's take a direct-response ad as an example. One simple way to test its effectiveness is through an A/B split run.

Many newspapers and magazines will allow you to run one ad in half of their issues and another in the other. For instance, you can code a display or mail-order advertisement by adding Department D to your phone number or address to gauge response. You can also test which media are pulling best for you by coding your ads via publication and date. If you run in the *Washington Post*, for example, the code printed in the coupon text of your ad might read WP 8/31. For easier evaluation, test one copy, headline, or offer element at a time. In his book *Tested Advertising Methods* (Prentice-Hall), advertising great John Caples reminds us to always test four factors when advertising in magazines, newspapers, or broadcast media:

1. Copy. What you say, your appeal, or promise, and how you express it.

2. Media. The magazines, newspapers, broadcasting facilities, and other vehicles that will carry your message.

3. Position. Where your ad appears in publications; what times during the day and what day of the week for broadcast messages.

4. Season. Which months are best.

When testing direct-mail letters and packages, here are the four key elements to test—in order of importance:

1. Your product or service

2. The list

3. Your offer

4. The copy

Of course there are many other variables you may need to test in your mailing pieces—like price, envelope size and color, teasers, letter length, lift letters, discount and credit terms, premiums, time limits, number of elements in the package, and so on. You have to decide which of these elements are important to test. Don't get so caught up in testing that you fail to roll out your promotion. Testing is designed to help you, not hinder you in getting your product or service into the hands of people who need it.

If your mailing is small (less than a thousand), if you're mailing to people who already know you, or if you're in a rush to take advantage of a time-sensitive opportunity, you can usually forgo testing. However, you would still want to bring in a copywriter or direct-response consultant to give you a second opinion on your marketing materials.

Once you know what works and what doesn't, you'll be able to hit the marketplace running with successful products, services, offers, and messages that you can profit from over and over again.

Caution: The Federal Trade Commission strictly limits testing

Hint One of the costliest mistakes you can make is prematurely changing your ad or direct-mail package because you get tired of it. Remember, you'll always get bored with your marketing before your target audience does. Why? You're focused on it and see it virtually every day, while your target audience only pays minimal attention.

a product or service that exists only in concept simply to gauge response. You must tell the prospect your product or service doesn't exist yet and you may not collect payment up front.

Two other eye-opening resources for testing and improving your mailings are René Gnam's *Direct Mail Workshop* (Prentice-Hall) and John Kremer's *Complete Direct Marketing Sourcebook* (John Wiley & Sons).

Strategy 13: Some Direct Advertising Options

Besides direct-mail letters and packages, you can reach people directly in a number of other ways, including space ads, classified ads, advertorials, postcards, and newsletters. The following examples will give you some idea of how to approach customers directly using these formats.

Small Space Ads: More Leads for Less $$$

Small space ads are smart, cost-effective tools for generating leads. You can arouse curiosity by offering people something to get them to phone, fax, or write you. Here's an example of a small space ad to get you started.

Of course you'll need to follow up these leads with a strong sales letter/response package.

Also consider low-cost classified space in newspapers, magazines, and industry newsletters on a local, regional, national, and international basis. Classified ads typically work best when targeted at business opportunity, automotive, real estate, and employment prospects.

If you're selling nationally through display and classified ads, you'll want to refer to the *Standard Rate and Data* books in your library for appropriate publications as well as the brokers who can save you money on larger media buys.

Extra! Extra! Editorial Ads Increase Readership

You see them all the time. Ads that don't look like ads but appear to be editorial copy or stories in the publication you're reading. Savvy marketers use this technique because they know people are five to nine times more likely to read editorial copy than a display ad. The *advertorial* (a hybrid of advertising and editorial) format works because readers perceive that your product or service is newsworthy. And with marketing, as with many things in life, perception is reality.

Advertorials are extremely effective as direct-response vehicles. But you will need to have a dashed border around a response coupon at the bottom of your ad or some kind of marching orders asking your prospects to write or phone. We've seen more and more businesses using this technique, but many are still not asking their prospects to do something! For examples of advertorials, look at *Success* and *Parade* magazines as well your trade publications.

Power-Packed Postcards = Low-Cost Profits

Postcards are cost-effective tools for reaching your target audience. Most advertisers don't sell directly from postcards, but use them as lead-generating devices. You can mail them yourself or, if you're selling nationally, through co-op card packs. If you're interested in card packs (the ones containing fifty to two hundred cards stacked and wrapped in cellophane),

Hint You may want to ask your advertising representative to place your advertorial ad inside an actual article. That way, the publication's editorial copy literally wraps around your ad and is virtually impossible to miss. The media won't always guarantee this placement, but you can request it.

simply head for your local library and ask to see the *Standard Rates and Data* book for card packs (the "big red one"). Inside, you'll see hundreds of card packs that reach horizontal markets (all types of businesses) or specific vertical markets like accountants, printers, attorneys, and more.

If you're mailing the postcards yourself, you may want to create a double postcard format with a first-class business-reply card attached so that your prospects can mail back their responses. For maximum productivity, you can even create a postcard containing a reply card and your Rolodex card for a three-in-one mailer! Just ask a printer about this.

For maximum productivity, you can even create a postcard containing a reply card and your Rolodex card for a three-in-one mailer!

Newsletters: Powerful Sales and Referral Tools

Newsletters are subtle yet seductive sales tools that help you stay connected with your target audiences. They reinforce the perception that you really know your business and that you care enough to communicate helpful advice on a regular basis.

Newsletter formats can range from one-page sheets mailed every quarter to multipage, multicolor monthly publications. For our purposes, we're talking about information-filled newsletters that you send to your prospects, clients, and the media on a regular basis, free of charge. Fresh story angles and a clean easy-to-read graphic design will increase readership. Plus, messages couched in an editorial format tend to achieve greater credibility and results. Try incorporating several of the following elements in your newsletter format to positively influence prospective customers and encourage customer retention.

New products
How-to articles
Client profiles
Personnel profiles
Your success stories
New industry trends
Pending legislation

New clients being served
Survey questionnaires/
    survey results
Quizzes
Reprints of feature articles
    relevant to your target
    audience

You'll also want to encourage reader response by keeping your newsletter interactive. Offer special promotions, contests, drawings, and advance-notice sales to increase letter, phone, and fax responses. If your budget allows, you may want to personalize your newsletter with electronic printing similar to a concept being used on magazine covers. Several marketers are reporting increased response by including their customers' or prospects' names inside articles and even cartoon balloons.

Strategy 14:
Word-of-Mouth Marketing

One of the fastest, least expensive, and most productive ways to generate new business is through referrals. When it comes to generating referrals, reality is irrelevant and perception is everything. People who give referrals are motivated by two primary factors: their perception of the value you've delivered and the level of rapport the two of you share. Unfortunately, if you're like many business-

> people, you probably take referrals for granted or on a
> catch-as-catch-can basis. You have no proactive plan for
> stimulating the maximum number of referrals.

Three Keys to Stimulating Maximum Referrals

1. EXCEED EXPECTATIONS. Whoever said "There's no traffic jam on the extra mile," knew the key to customer satisfaction and obtaining abundant referrals. We have to earn our referrals. Always under-promise and over-deliver because inspired customers refer liberally. Give them something they didn't expect. Is it a free analysis of their insurance? A free book? Let them know you're giving this gift to welcome them to your practice or business or for their loyal patronage. Give them thirteen instead of the twelve they expect. It's important to communicate the value they are receiving so they appreciate the extras even more.

2. ASK FOR REFERRALS. To get referrals, you must overcome askaphobia. Does asking mean you need business? Actually, 99 percent of the time it's a thought that crosses only your mind! People want to help you. But you've got to ask! Here are several ways to go about it:

➡ "I'd like to ask you for a favor. If you've liked what I've done for you here, I'd like you to send me someone I can help the same way I've helped you. I'm sure they'll be pleased."

➡ "Who else do you know who may benefit from my service?"

➡ "Would you be kind enough to give me the names of two or three people who may be interested in (solving this problem) (acquiring more customers) (our product) (our service)?"

3. SAY THANK YOU. It's human nature to take good things for granted. Always show appreciation to your clients and customers for their business and referrals with thank-you notes, gifts, free consulting, services, or cash.

Referral Letters and Coupons

Create a letter or postcard that rewards your customers for referring others to you. It would go something like this: "You made a smart move when you selected Allegro Bank's Moneyline personal credit service. Now go ahead and make another smart move by telling a friend. As soon as they open a Moneyline, you receive $50. To make it easy for you, I've enclosed five Moneyline Tell-a-Friend coupons. Just complete side A of each coupon and give them to your friends and family."

Conduct Referral Promotions

Give your customers cards, coupons, or certificates good for gifts or discounts that they can endorse like a check and give to their friends and colleagues. Then give away

---

Do a Friend a Favor!

THIS COUPON IS FOR A FRIEND OR RELATIVE

$12 OFF

Your Dry Cleaning at Crescent Cleaners with a minimum order of $30.

We're located in the Fall Manor Shopping Center, 15250 Georgia Avenue. Come in or call 942-0000 for FREE Pickup & Delivery!

Give this coupon to a friend or relative and they will receive $12 off their dry cleaning. And to say thanks, we'll give you $12 more of FREE dry cleaning with your minimum order of $30! Just sign your name below so we can give you the proper credit on your order.

NAME _____ is entitled to $12 of FREE dry cleaning for passing this card along to a friend or relative who becomes our customer.

Expires 8-15-97

---

prizes or rewards to those who generate the most referrals within a certain period. Don't forget to promote these programs in your mailers and with your employees.

Endorsed Testimonial/Referral Letter

The key in using referral letters is to send the letters to the circle of influencers or champions of the person giving the referral, as well as to your own prospects. Be sure it is written on the referrer's letterhead and includes that person's signature. On pages 90–92 is a letter that was sent out by one of my clients to help promote my consulting business.

Another way to drum up referrals is to conduct referral events like open houses, business anniversary parties, free seminars, and luncheon meetings.

Rolodex parties also serve this purpose. Sit down with a friend, colleague, or business associate and call people you know on their behalf, while they call people they know on your behalf.

Offer Referral Fees

The potential of this strategy depends on the legalities of your business or industry. One of the best ways to get new business is to offer referral fees. By offering people generous incentives, you'll get plenty of business. Also, if you do get a qualified referral, make sure you pay the referrer immediately. On page 93 is a flier I use to consistently generate attention and get results for my speaking, training,

Andrew G. Anderson

Attorney At Law

345 Reed Street

Silver Spring, MD 20906

Tel: 301-554-7744 * Fax: 301-554-7755

"Have you read a book you just couldn't put down? I did. But it wasn't written by Michael Crichton, Stephen King, or Tom Clancy. It was authored by an amazing marketing consultant who has changed my business life forever!"

Dear Colleague,

Until recently, my practice was exploding. My staff and I could hardly keep up with the crush of new refinancing business. Then, interest rates rose and my flood of business dried up. I realized I'd made a classic business blunder. I stopped marketing when the sun was shining. And when the dark clouds blew in, I was scrambling for new business.

Fortunately, I discovered a book co-written by Dan McComas, a marketing consultant, copywriter, and sales trainer. I literally couldn't put it down and it's no understatement to say that it has transformed my career and practice virtually overnight! Through his book, Marketing Boot Camp, Dan taught me how to recognize and optimize many of the areas and opportunities available from my practice that I'd simply overlooked or never considered.

I'm pretty good at one-on-one meetings. Yet when it came to marketing or persuading the entire marketplace to see and then seize our advantages, I realized I needed help. That's when I called Dan and hired him as my personal marketing coach. Now, in just several months together, I've had my most profitable two months of the year . . . EVER!

Are you consistently challenged to grow your marketing potential?

If you're a business owner, consultant, or sales professional, you probably don't have anyone to really challenge you to maximize your actions and results. That is, to advise you on what you're doing right, what you're doing wrong, and what you're not doing that you should be. Well, as my challenger, Dan has gotten me so fired up I'm really enjoying my business again! His methods have made it more pleasant to market because I'm no longer selling. I'm helping people succeed.

For example, Dan has drilled into my brain the concept of GIVING back to my clients and prospects. Simply put, when you give, you get. Dan has helped me implement two powerful strategies that have brought about <u>immediate</u> new business:

1. I'm giving away copies of his book <u>Marketing Boot Camp</u> as a gift to Realtors and mortgage brokers. They have all expressed genuine gratitude that I want to help them succeed, and the payback in new business is coming in faster than I'd imagined.

2. I've bought airtime on a local business radio station to promote Realtors on my <u>Real Estate Review</u> show. Hardly anyone presents opportunities like this to their prospects and clients. Why can't you? Like any consultant worth his salt, Dan helps me to <u>capitalize</u> on opportunities I knew existed but couldn't find the time or focus to implement. Sometimes we <u>all</u> need a kick in the pants to reach that next level!

I've also learned that to sustain marketing success, you must have a well-structured system in place. Dan teaches you how to <u>differentiate</u> and <u>systematize</u> your business better and more effectively than you are now. One of his key principles is developing relationships with your prospects and clients through better networking, referral-building, and ongoing promotional letters. He's also a master copywriter and is helping me improve my ads, brochures, and news releases.

One of the areas we're aggressively pursuing is generating publicity. Why? Because business today has no other leverage left except to distinguish itself through innovation and promotion. Most businesses, after all, have been reduced to carbon-copy commodities. No one can buy a product or service that much better than anyone else's (at least in the consumer's mind!). How do you overcome this? Through powerful promotion and information campaigns that educate and position you and your company as one who adds a greater, more decisive <u>value perception</u> to what you are marketing.

Why am I sharing these insights with you?

First, it's part of my personal philosophy of giving. I'm so sold on Dan's personal coaching and marketing methods that I wanted to tell you about them. I truly believe his advice will benefit anyone he works with. If you're fortunate enough to become his client, I believe you too will be very pleased with the results. You can reach him at 301-946-6636 for a free, no-obligation consultation. Or, fill out the coupon and mail or fax it to him—and good luck!

Sincerely yours,

Andy Anderson
Attorney At Law

- Clip Here -

YES, Dan—I want my prospects to BUY NOW and my clients to BUY AGAIN FAST! Tell me more about your personal executive coaching, marketing consulting, copywriting, graphic design, and customized training for business owners, managers, professionals, and salespeople. The best time to call is _____.

Name _____   Title _____

Address _____   Phone _____

City _____   State _____ Zip _____

Dan McComas | Author * Speaker * Seminar Leader * Marketing and Sales Strategist
11409 Catalina Terrace | Silver Spring, MD 20902 | 301-946-6636 | Fax: 301-946-6910 | e-mail: promocoach@aol.com

---

copywriting, and coaching business. (P.S. The offer on the flier is still good!)

According to Arnold Sanow, my *Marketing Boot Camp* co-author, to make sure your referral fee program works, follow these guidelines:

Make $500 or More for Just a Few Minutes' Work!

REFERRAL OPPORTUNITY #1: If you know a meeting planner, training director, human resources director, personnel director, association contact, or <u>anyone</u> who hires speakers and trainers . . . then you have the opportunity to make BIG $$$$ right now! We offer customized training programs, seminars, and keynote speeches in the following areas: <u>Secrets of Marketing and Publicity on a Low Budget</u>, <u>Marketing Your Professional Services</u>, <u>Network Your Way to Success</u>, <u>Unlock Your Creative Genius</u>, <u>How to Write the Million-Dollar Sales Letter</u>, <u>Exceptional Customer Service</u>, and <u>How to Make Powerful Presentations</u>.

REFERRAL OPPORTUNITY #2: If you know a business owner, marketing and sales executive, graphic designer, newsletter publisher, association executive, or anyone who hires marketing strategists and copywriters for ads, fliers, sales letters, brochures, news releases, annual reports, and articles . . . then you have the opportunity to make $$$$ right now, too!

By referring us to those people in your network who hire speakers, trainers, and copywriters, you will receive 10 percent of all the money we get from our speaking, training, and writing fees, PLUS you will also receive 10 percent of all the money we make from our product sales.

<u>"We have all of the materials and winning testimonials to close the sale. If you have one lead or many, don't miss this unique opportunity to earn big $$$ for just a few minutes' work!"</u>

Please feel free to contact us at:

Dan McComas Associates | Business Development & Training | 301-946-6636

➨ Pay referrers immediately. Don't make them wait and, above all, don't make them chase you down to get their referral fee.

➨ Let referrers know that if any other business comes from the client they referred, you will give them a referral fee for the next year.

➨ Put the referral flier on bulletin boards, use it as a leave-behind at events or as an insert in newsletters, and give it out at seminars where you speak.

A Six-Step Process That Gets Referrals Every Time

Here is an excerpt from my interview with America's Referral Coach, Bill Cates:

Dan McComas: Bill, you've developed a very effective model for asking clients for referrals. Let's explore your process.

Bill Cates: Sure, and thanks for letting me help your readers. Your first step is to treat the asking with reverence. First, make sure you create enough time to have a conversation with your client about referrals. Gain enough time for the appointment and manage your time on the appointment so your request isn't rushed at the end.

Second, open up with a statement such as, "Bob, I have a very important question I've been meaning to ask you." This will get their attention and show them this is important to you. If you feel awkward about asking for referrals, you won't treat the asking with reverence, yet since this is the most important of steps, you must over-come your awkwardness.

DM: How do you do that?

BC: There are many barriers you may face in asking for referrals. You might be afraid of jeopardizing the relationship and future sales. You might feel you haven't served the prospect or customer enough (so you don't deserve to ask). You might hear "no" and think it means more than it does. Many people don't ask because they've had a bad experience with referrals and they don't want that to happen to their clients.

It usually boils down to the F word . . . FEAR. Fear of rejection, or the fear that asking for referrals will somehow damage the relationship you have with your satisfied client. Like most fears, this one is a ghost. In fact, it's really a projection onto your potential referral source. It's a trick your unconscious mind plays on you. Since you're feeling awkward about asking for referrals, you think the other person will feel awkward about being asked.

If you've done your best to be sincere, if you've served them well, and if you've established a relationship of mutual trust, then your clients and referral alliances will not mind your request. In fact, they may be extremely happy to help you. Remember to foreshadow your request for referrals early on in the relationship; then it will be much easier for you to ask. The truth is, because referrals allow you to serve many people your clients know, the referral process can actually strengthen your relationships with your clients.

DM: That's great! What's next?

BC: Third, You need to ask for their help. You know, all successful people in this world have learned that it's a sign of high self-esteem to be able to ask for help. If you are serving your clients well . . . if they like you and trust you . . . they'll probably be happy to help you—you just have to ask. I use the phrase, "I'm trying to expand my business and I need your help." It's a phrase that's worked well for me. Lately I've been saying, "I'm trying to build my business and I value your help." I'm still asking for help, but the word "value" is also a show of respect for them. I ask for referrals and honor my client at the same time.

DM: In your book *Unlimited Referrals*, you talk about the importance of explaining the referral process. Why is this important?

BC: Before I engage my client in exploring who they know, I usually explain what will happen if she gives me a referral. If I found her through a referral, I'll remind her of how I contacted her. Then I'll say something like, "If you choose to refer someone to me, I'll ask you to call them first, just to let them know why I'm calling. They'll probably appreciate a call from you, someone they know." Whatever your process for contacting your new prospect, let your client know that it will be professional and you won't become a pest.

DM: All right, now we're cooking. Let's explore step 4.

BC: The fourth step is to gain permission to explore. This is important because you want to have a conversation that allows you to have some influence on the quality of referrals you receive. It's also important so both you and your client feel comfortable in the conversation. Try saying something like, "I was wondering if we could explore who you know who might benefit from the type of work I do. Are you comfortable with that?"

Another approach might be, "Barbara, let's brainstorm for a minute on how I might be able to help someone you know. Could we do that for a minute?" If you gain their permission to have this conversation, you'll feel more comfortable in the process and you'll probably get much higher quality referrals.

DM: One problem with getting referrals is that blank stare you get after you ask someone if they know anyone they can refer us to. How do you overcome this, Bill?

BC: It's best that you don't throw open the entire universe for them to consider with a statement like, "Who do you know—" It's more effective to help them picture a smaller group of people in their world. If you know they're active in their church, temple, or Chamber of Commerce, you can start there.

Here, then, is the fifth step in getting referrals. If you're looking for clients who fit a specific profile, share that profile with your referral source. You may not get as many referrals, but the ones you do get will be just what you're looking for.

DM: Do you prefer quality or quantity referrals?

BC: As you begin to ask on a more regular basis, you'll notice that many of your clients will begin to think of several people all at once. Let them free-associate for a few minutes. Record the names. Then go back to learn more about each one.

Don't be surprised when one of your clients pulls out a directory for their association or club. When this happens to me, I try to help them focus on three to five quality referrals. I tell them I'll be back for more later. To me, quality is more important than quantity.

Your sixth and final action step should be to put this model to work. I suggest you begin with the client who loves you the most. You can bumble through this process and still get a great referral. You'll have a success, you'll refine your approach, and then you can move on to those clients who simply like you.

Bill Cates is America's Referral Coach and the author of Unlimited Referrals: Secrets That Turn Your Business Relationships into Gold *(Thunder Hill Press, 1996; 800-488-5464).*

Expanding Your Sphere of Influence

We all know roughly 250 people. Of that number, an American Management Association survey says that approximately fifty-two of these people are potential referral sources for our business. Most entrepreneurs and professionals do not maximize referral opportunities. To discipline your referral thinking, write out a list of twenty people who could refer warm or hot new business prospects to you. Don't forget that givers get, and the best way to get referrals is to give them to others.

Ask yourself these questions: Who do I know? Who knows me? Use the list below as your referral jumpstarter. Take ten minutes and quickly begin listing names. Try not to judge the person's potential as you write, since this will only block your flow. I guarantee you'll be astonished at the number of possible referrers you generate. Let the list cool for a few hours or for a day and go back

To discipline your referral thinking, write out a list of twenty people who could refer warm or hot new business prospects to you.

over it to prioritize names. Even if you come up with only five valid referral sources out of twenty, you're way ahead of the game.

Here is a list of potential referrers followed by a write-in section to get you started:

Clients	Church members
Former clients	Civic/Charitable
Business associates	Recreation
Social club members	Creditors
Business club members	Employees
Chambers of Commerce	College connections
Rotary and other clubs	High school connections
Vendors	Association members
Friends	Family members

1. _____   11. _____
2. _____   12. _____
3. _____   13. _____
4. _____   14. _____
5. _____   15. _____
6. _____   16. _____
7. _____   17. _____
8. _____   18. _____
9. _____   19. _____
10. _____   20. _____

Generate New and Repeat Business and Referrals

Everyone is walking around with signs on their backs saying, "Make me feel important, make me feel special." The following client (and prospect) retention strategies and tools will ensure an easier path of doing business and help you effectively develop and cement profitable long-term relationships.

Relationship Reinforcers You Can Mail or Fax

- ➡ Article in which you're mentioned
- ➡ Article published by you
- ➡ White-paper on issue of interest
- ➡ Practice area primer
- ➡ Transcript from a seminar
- ➡ Testimonial letter from satisfied client
- ➡ Tickets to a ball game, seminar, or special event
- ➡ Newsletter
- ➡ Firmwide or practice area brochure
- ➡ Q&A sheet to preempt frequently asked questions
- ➡ Case study of problem you've solved that your contact is experiencing
- ➡ Survey results by you or others
- ➡ Articles on business trends affecting your target audience
- ➡ Articles of special personal interest to your contact with a personal note
- ➡ Postcard from business trip or vacation
- ➡ Relevant news releases, announcements of new services, or special promotions
- ➡ Holiday, birthday, or thank-you cards
- ➡ A "thanks for the business or referral" gift basket, plant, or personal gift
- ➡ A professional or personal book (lend or send)
- ➡ Survey to ask clients how you can improve

Face-to-Face Relationship Reinforcers

➡ Host a meeting, lunch-and-learn seminar, or mini-training session at your office.

➡ Host a meeting, seminar, or mini-training session at your contact's site.

➡ Offer a new business referral.

➡ Invite contact to sports event, speech, etc.

➡ Share a cab to the airport or a meeting.

➡ Exercise together.

➡ Invite contact to sit with you at a meeting or event.

➡ Host an open house at your home or office.

➡ Invite contact to volunteer for civic project with you.

➡ Teach a course (publicize it to contacts).

➡ Speak or sit on panels at chamber and association meetings.

➡ Join networking groups where your ideal clients are members.

➡ Volunteer for leadership role in networking and association groups.

➡ Start your own networking or referral club.

➡ Suggest a power breakfast or lunch.

➡ Visit a good contact or client in the hospital; don't just send flowers.

➡ Interview your contact for a speech or article you're writing.

Think of it this way. How many of these kinds of thoughtful communications do you receive from the people you give your business to? The answer—probably not many. Remember, givers gain. Why not take the initiative to nurture lasting and productive relationships that will pay dividends that compound annually for a long, long time?

Strategy 15: Visibility and Credibility Through Free Publicity

It's been said that advertising is what you pay for, publicity is what you pray for. To have your prayers answered, you must think of PR not just as a press release, but as a process that helps you educate, inform, and persuade your target audiences. This requires patient relationship building with the media. Like your targeted customer prospects, these journalists must get to know and trust you before you become an information or quotable resource. Give the media what they want and, in all likelihood, you'll get the consistent exposure you want and need to grow your business. Better still, publicity costs less and provides more credibility than you could ever achieve with paid advertising.

Get Your Share of the Free Publicity Pie

What do newspaper, magazine, trade publication, and newsletter editors and television and radio producers want? They're hungry for news, how-to articles, new services, new product releases, and human interest stories to

Give the media what they want and, in all likelihood, you'll get the consistent exposure you want and need to grow your business.

keep their readers and listeners informed and entertained. Eighty percent of the stories you see and hear every day in the print and electronic media have been provided or planted by companies and PR firms who know how to work with the appropriate media.

Positive publicity is one of the most powerful ways to reach, influence, and motivate your prospects and customers to trust that your product or service can help them. That's because people tend to believe what they see and hear in the media. It's always more credible to have a third party say good things about you than to blow your own horn. Think of the media not so much as a group, but as individual editors, reporters, and broadcasters with one purpose: to educate, entertain, and offer news to their readers, listeners, and viewers. If you can help them accomplish this while making it easy for them to use your information, they'll consistently look to you as a resource.

The media are interested in many types of communications from your company. Here's a sampling of the subjects you can offer to establish yourself as a valuable resource:

➡ Company, individual, or product success stories
➡ Case histories of successful services and products and how people are using them
➡ New products or services
➡ Executive appointments and promotions
➡ New clients
➡ Research/industry forecasts and trends
➡ Survey results
➡ Community involvement

It's always more credible to have a third party say good things about you than to blow your own horn.

➡ Trade shows

➡ Free reports

➡ Feature releases

➡ Company anniversary

One-on-one meetings and editorial tours of your company with local and regional editors are excellent ways to build relationships with the media. Another effective tool for working with industry publications is to create and submit a camera-ready feature story. You'd be surprised how many periodicals will pick up a well-written, ready-to-go article. Why? It offers news or value to their readers and it's incredibly easy for the editor to use!

Here are some general tips for working effectively with reporters and editors:

1. Keep an updated press file in your database similar to your prospect/customer file. Change is a constant for media people, so you must stay on top of this. Be sure to target "influencer" publication/stations and a list of journalists with whom you can establish in-depth relationships.

2. Find a hook, angle, or unusual twist to your story. "Man Bites Dog" always gets more press or air time than "Dog Bites Man." Use the creativity techniques we recommend in this book to brainstorm unique approaches.

3. Timing is everything. Tie your story to a particular season,

Hint Especially with new product introductions, it's a good idea to include the cost of the product in your news release as well as how and where to get it.

event, holiday, or national news story. A recent article in the business section of the *Washington Post* revealed that most Americans are in the dark about how to manage their money and investments. This is a perfect opportunity for a financial planner to send out a news release with a headline saying: "According to a Recent Survey Conducted by [the source], 9 out of 10 Americans Have Absolutely No Idea How to Manage Their Investments. Are You One of Them?" Then, in the news release, offer a free booklet titled *10 Simple Strategies for Managing and Generating Higher Returns on Your Personal Investments* and just wait for the phone to ring.

4. Make your press release, how-to article, or feature story factual. There's a fine line to walk between facts and promotional copy but one thing is certain: Editors will "round file" anything that smacks of hype or extravagance. It's not their job to promote your company. Remember, you're not offering news or information to them per se, but to their readers and listeners.

5. Meet deadlines. Regrettably, many publicity opportunities are lost every day because an individual or company missed a media deadline. Be sure to ask each publication or station for its editorial calendar and deadlines. Also, when speaking to a reporter, your first question should be, "Are you on deadline?" If the answer is yes, quickly ask when you can return the call, thank the reporter, and hang up. Many editors and reporters don't work 9-to-5 jobs, so you must be available day or night when they need a quote or have a question.

6. Call editors with your story ideas. Due to multiple deadline pressures, media people need reminder

calls. Once you've submitted an article or news release you've discussed with an editor, feel free to call to see if he or she has received it and if there are any questions. Don't call to ask if they've picked up or used your release. That's a dead giveaway that you don't read their publication or listen to or watch their shows.

Tips for Writing a Winning News Release

➥ Write the release on your letterhead with the word "NEWS."

➥ Depending upon your timing, include the date you would like your news released or write "For Immediate Release" if it can be used upon receipt.

➥ Include your name or your contact's name and phone (both office and home phone, since reporters work around the clock). Be available and sensitive to their deadlines.

➥ Double-space your typed story so editors can make notes. Avoid typos.

➥ Put your most important information (what? who? when? where? how?) in the headline and lead paragraph. Editors cut from the bottom up.

➥ Avoid adjectives and hype—this is not ad writing but fact writing. Be specific.

➥ Back it up with quotes and statistics whenever possible. Quotes are a great way to make a strong statement about your product or service without sounding like a commercial. Plus, quotes liven up a news release.

➡ Type ### or —END— when finished.

Free Publicity . . . Your Best Publicity

Radio and television stations, newspapers, and magazines are always looking for guests. Every day, thousands of guests are needed throughout the United States. And the media are looking for entrepreneurs and executives like you! The reason free publicity on radio, on television, and in print works better than paid advertisements is the credibility factor. When people see or hear you on a talk show or read about you in print, their perception is that your company must know its business. To help you get booked on radio and television shows or to get your articles published, you'll want to investigate the resources that follow. The first three may either be purchased or found in your local library.

Here's an effective resource to help you identify and contact 1,591 daily newspapers, 13,848 weekly newspapers, and 9,677 trade/consumer magazines and newsletters. Bacon's also publishes lists for radio and television stations. **Bacon's Publicity Checker, Bacon's Publishing Company, 332 S. Michigan Ave., Chicago, IL 60604; 312-922-2400.**

For listings of 1,627 daily and 5,867 weekly newspapers, 235 magazines, 430 trade magazines, 2,820 professional business publications, and many radio and television stations, you will also want to consider:

When people see or hear you on a talk show or read about you in print, their perception is that your company must know its business.

All-in-One Directory, Gebbie Press, P.O. Box 1000, New Paltz, NY 12561; 914-255-7560.

More than 20,000 specialized newsletter publishers are eager to hear from you, too. One of the best resources for identifying and contacting the publications that target your audiences is: **Oxbridge Dictionary of Newsletters, Oxbridge Communications, 150 Fifth Ave., Suite 302, New York, NY 10011; 212-741-0231.**

For a database of 20,000 media contacts (all types), call Open Horizons toll-free at 800-796-6130. With this database, you can target media by subject interest, location, or the kinds of items they like to cover. This database is especially valuable for selecting and targeting those top media that you want to add to your 9/18 Relationship Marketing System database for press releases.

For a *Do-It-Yourself Publicity Kit* that includes many examples of how to write a news release as well as many samples of feature releases, author bios, fact sheets, Q&As, and other items that you might want to include in your media kit, contact **Open Horizons, P.O. Box 205, Fairfield, IA 52556-0205; 515-472-6130 or 800-796-6130; fax: 515-472-1560; e-mail: *info@bookmarket*; Web: *http://www.bookmarket.com*.** This kit also includes many more directories and other resources to help you publicize your products and services.

For your press release planning, you'll want to consult *Marketing Made Easier, Guide to Free Publicity* by Barry Klein (Todd Publications). All the information has been organized to provide you with valuable shortcuts to find the print sources that match your product or publicity needs. The directory is divided into two parts: alphabetical—with listings of more than 1,000 magazines, newsletters, and trade publications; and by target index—containing approximately 120 target audiences matched to specific publications serving that particular audience. Call 301-946-6636 for details.

If you have a book or information product to sell and are looking for a low-cost publicity strategy for promoting it, you may want to contact our friend Joe Sabah. Joe and his wife, Judy, self-publish a book titled *How to Get the Job You Really Want and Get Employers to Call You.* They've sold more than 19,000 copies almost exclusively through national talk radio programs from in-home telephone interviews, and Joe has created a step-by-step system and a list of stations to help anyone do this. You can reach him at **Pacesetter Publications, P.O. Box 101330, Denver, CO 80250; 303-722-7200.**

For about $10, the *United Way Media Fact Book* lists every TV and radio station, newspaper, and magazine in most cities. Just give the United Way in your area a call.

For a small fee you can put your ad into the *Directory of Experts, Authorities and Spokespersons.* It's distributed to almost every television station, radio station, magazine, and newspaper throughout the United States. When someone needs a guest, there's a good chance they'll look up someone like you. For more information, call the publisher, Mitch Davis, at 800-YEARBOOK (800-932-7266).

Your Credentials Kit

Your prospects need *proof* that you, your product, or your service can help them solve a problem or realize a gain.

And your customers, clients, and patients need constant reassurance to remain loyal. Consider using a two-pocket folder to house your materials. Here are key items that you might want to include in your credentials kit:

- Business card
- Rolodex card
- Biographies of key individuals in your company or association
- Article reprints written by you
- Articles written about you
- Your newsletter
- Pricing or fee schedules (if applicable)
- Testimonial sheet (showing multiple testimonials)
- Individual testimonials on client letterhead
- Business and trade organizations
- Expert or celebrity endorsements
- References—the more the better
- Audio- or videotapes
- Before and after photos
- Q&A sheet
- List of clients or customers
- Your cover letter to the prospect or media
- A menu of services you offer
- Guarantees and warranties
- Credentials—academic, awards, affiliations
- Case studies or success stories
- Brochure

How much proof is enough? Marketing expert Dan Kennedy said it best: "You can *never* have enough proof."

So keep those articles and testimonials flowing to bolster your value perception in the eyes of your prospects and clients.

How to Write a Business How-To Article and Get It Published

People are hungry for information. Why? Because they want to solve their problems or improve their lot. That means editors and reporters are always looking for advice that informs and entertains their readers. What you must do is convince the editor that your article will meet these requirements. And with so many newspapers, magazines, business publications, and industry newsletters, it's not difficult. What do you write about? For our purposes, let's assume you've never done this before.

The point is to provide enough (but not too much) information to assist people with the task at hand and, more importantly, to be perceived as a helpful or specialized problem-solver.

   1. The Topic. Select a topic that offers helpful advice or information. A plumber could title an article "The Easiest Way to Install a New Sink." An accountant might write about "5 Tips to Help You Pay Hundreds—Even Thousands—Less to Uncle Sam." Look at the headline samples in this book to jump-start your thinking. The point is to provide enough (but not too much) information to assist people with the task at hand and, more importantly, to be perceived as a helpful or specialized problem-solver. If you're at a loss for a topic or background material, gather your company's or industry's current marketing materials. Chances are you can adapt or structure your message around that copy.

2.   The Length. Before you begin writing you must know the length and types of articles used by the publication. Most how-to articles are 250, 500, 1,000, or 2,500 words.

3.   Use a Numbered Sequence. The easiest, fastest way to write a how-to article is with a sequenced structure like "10 Ways to—," "The 5 Inside Secrets of," "25 Ways to Improve Customer Service," etc.

4.   Start Writing and Keep Writing. Remember, there's a big difference between writing and editing. Don't try to edit as you write. Why? Because that little negative voice inside your head will start saying things like, "What? Who are *you* to write an article?" or "You see, I *knew* you couldn't write, just look at that grammar," or "Hey, your spelling's atrocious!" The best way to defeat these mental blocks (which reside in all of us to one degree or another) is to write. Write. Write. Write! Don't stop until you've exhausted your ideas. Even if you run out of inspiration keep your fingers moving on the keyboard and type something like *hdriertnasdsfie blah-blah-dum-te-dum ad-herfvnfkjiri*—until more ideas surface. And they will! Now . . . read it over. Don't worry about grammar, structure, logical sequence, or spelling. You can take care of that in the editing stage. Finally, walk away from it for a day and let your unconscious mind (the most creative part) take over. During the next twenty-four hours you'll come up with even more ideas and better ways to communicate them. You'll want to have a tape recorder or notepad by your bed to capture these brainstorms—some will be brilliant and some laughable. Now incorporate this ad-

Remember, there's a big difference between writing and editing. Don't try to edit as you write.

ditional information, look at your article with fresh eyes, and begin editing and polishing. In some paragraphs you'll be making wholesale changes; in others it will just be a matter of fine-tuning. Perhaps you've heard the truism that writing is 1 percent inspiration and 99 percent perspiration. It's true. Rewriting is key.

5. Use a Photo. Remember to include a 5 × 7-inch glossy black-and-white photo headshot when you send off your article. Many publications will use them.

Congratulations. You're an author! Feels great, doesn't it?

Caution: Never write an article that reads like a commercial for you or your company. Your target audience will never see it because the editor will never print it.

There are several strategies for approaching a reporter or editor. The fastest way is to call first and present your article idea. Editors are busy, so be sure to immediately explain how it will help their readers. Another way is to mail a query letter (with or without your article) and follow up with a phone call. Also, you should get a copy of the publication's editorial calendar to tie your future articles to seasonal or special theme editions.

In most cases, you won't get paid for these articles. But that's not your intention. You see, you're going to request that the publication run your biography or resource

Hint You may want to try this time-saving technique. Some writers find that dictating their article into a tape recorder and then transcribing the material is an efficient way to work.

box at the end of the article. What's a biography or re-source box? It's a mini-advertisement about you and your problem-solving expertise that provides a vehicle for your readers to connect with you. It might say "Jim Smith is a CPA and partner in the firm of Smith, Lambert and Jenkins based in Charlottesville, VA. His firm specializes in saving small-business owners money on their taxes. For a free copy of his *Business Owners: Never Pay More Than You Have To* kit, call Jim at 804-992-5780."

Now your readers have a reason to contact you. Trade publications and newsletters will typically run your bio box as you present it. However, most newspapers will only run your name, title, company name, and city. Oh yes, remember to include copyright information (© 1994 by Jim Smith) at the bottom of your article to automatically copyright your work.

Yes, people will read your by-lined article and compliment you and it will feel good. You'll also get calls that may result in new busi-ness. But the largest leverage you'll receive is by photocopying or reprint-ing your article and mailing it to your prospects and clients with a hand-written note that says, "Thought you'd be interested in my recently published article on how to (whatever

Hint If you don't have the time or inclination to write an article yourself, you can use a busi-ness freelance writer to ghost-write it for you. Simply have him or her interview you over the phone or in person. Don't fret over this method. After all, they are <u>your</u> ideas and many busy people do this. Just call your local Chamber of Commerce for a referral, place an ad in the paper, or look under <u>copywriter</u> or <u>writer</u> in the yellow pages.

your article was about)." You can also bind the article into proposals and use it as a handout at speaking engagements or civic, association, and chamber meetings. It's a powerful business-building tool that you can keep in your company's marketing arsenal and your personal propaganda package for years.

Sample Query Letter

Here is a sample query letter you can adapt for your purposes.

Dear (Editor's Name):

Small businesses are paying more taxes than they have to. Every day we help our clients (many of them your readers) save hundreds or even thousands of dollars simply by making small adjustments in their accounting procedures. That's why I wrote 5 Little-Known Accounting Secrets That Can Save Your Business Hundreds—Even Thousands—of Dollars Every Year.

A five-hundred-word article on the premise behind my book is enclosed for your review. (Or, "I have an article idea that . . . .") I believe it would be of great interest and benefit to your readers during the busy tax months of February and March.

I will call you shortly to gauge your interest.

Sincerely,

Jim Smith, CPA

P.S. By way of introduction, I've owned my CPA firm for twelve years. I have more than fifteen hundred clients and four associates working with me.

Strategy 16: Ignite Your Creative Fires

Einstein said, "Imagination is more powerful than knowledge." That goes double for advertising and marketing because innovation and excitement sell! That means you need to constantly create new and better ways to get your prospects' attention and to motivate them to try your product or service. Of course, stretching your creative problem-solving capabilities can help you solve virtually any challenge ranging from raising capital to training employees.

The problem is, most people believe they somehow missed the divine creative gene. Is this you? Well, get over it! Creative thinking is not limited to artists and inventors. You're more creative than you may believe. We guarantee it. You just need an open mind and several of the following idea-generating techniques. But beware. Solving marketing challenges or any problem without a strategy is like shooting arrows wearing a blindfold. To find the right answers, you have to ask the right questions.

Before you tackle any marketing challenge, you should work hand in hand with the Nineteen Crucial Questions discussed in Success Strategy 9. This list helps you focus on how your product, service, publication, or institution will be meaningfully communicated to consumers' needs, wants, desires, and dreams. Your big ideas must be relevant to this strategy to be successful. Advertising great David Ogilvy put it best when he said, "If it doesn't sell, it ain't creative."

Stretching your creative problem-solving capabilities can help you solve virtually any challenge ranging from raising capital to training employees.

Ideas are organic. They're all around us. What we need are techniques to spark our creative fires. Here are several methods that work for us and can work for you:

Mind Mapping

Also known as clustering, this nonlinear brainstorming process is used to override the "that's a stupid idea" logical left side of your brain with intuitive, right-brained associations emanating from personal experience. On a fresh page, circle a nucleus word or phrase. Write down any connections that relate to the nucleus word as quickly as you can. Circle the new words or phrases and draw lines to related patterns. When you free-associate from one idea to another, you'll experience a chain reaction that can create an explosion of new thought patterns and ideas. Mind mapping is a revealing exercise that will help you develop numerous emotion-based ideas. And emotion sells!

Forced Relationships

Try to force two seemingly unrelated things or ideas. Pet rocks, Mickey Mouse, and clock radios are examples of this technique.

Make the Familiar Strange, the Strange Familiar

Remember the '60s Volkswagen ad headline that trumpeted "Lemon?" It was really an ad for quality control

When you free-associate from one idea to another, you'll experience a chain reaction that can create an explosion of new thought patterns and ideas.

that helped sell thousands of Beetles. You can also put a spin on clichés, catch phrases, and idioms, rework famous quotes, and incorporate irony and metaphor in your creative thinking and writing. Can you take your product or service and shrink it, stretch it, turn it upside down, communicate the opposite?

Brainstorming

One of the best ways to arrive at a winning creative solution is to generate a ton of ideas by brainstorming with a group or by yourself. One brainstorming path you can take is down the One Hundred Ideas road. Coming up with a hundred ideas for a product, problem, or headline is really not as difficult as it sounds. And while you're producing so many ideas you can tap into your unconscious mind, which, when uninterrupted by any negative voice of judgment, will yield far more interesting and effective solutions than if you stopped at idea No. 12. Don't worry. Suspend judgment. Let go. Wild off-the-wall thoughts are OK, too! Finally, after you generate an avalanche of ideas, you must decisively cull them into a single interesting, compelling, and effective solution.

Idea Bank

Keep an idea bank or swipe file of words, phrases, ads, brochures, and sales letters that have gotten your attention to help spark new ideas through lateral thinking. Good ideas come at the strangest time—usually when you're not consciously thinking about your challenge (how many ah-ha's have come to you in the shower, for example?). Don't forget to carry a tape recorder (or keep one on your nightstand) and index cards to capture your magic moments. Napkins, candy bar wrappers, and restaurant placemats work quite well in a pinch!

Never underestimate the powerful potential of your creativity. Always challenge yourself to sidestep shopworn solutions. The sheer joy of the creative process is rewarding in itself. The icing on the cake is that monetary rewards tend to follow those who can solve problems in original ways. We wish you much spontaneous combustion!

Following are samples of big creative ideas that have earned billions for these advertisers. They seem so simple, but you can bet your briefcase that hundreds to thousands of hours and ideas were brainstormed to come up with these profitable gems:

> **The sheer joy of the creative process is rewarding in itself. The icing on the cake is that monetary rewards tend to follow those who can solve problems in original ways.**

Greyhound: "Leave the Driving to Us"

Maxwell House: "Good to the Last Drop"

Federal Express: "When It Absolutely, Positively Has to Be There Overnight"

Clairol: "Does She or Doesn't She?"

Kodak Film: "A Kodak Moment"

"Marlboro Country"

American Express Travelers Checks: "Don't Leave Home Without Them"

Purdue Chicken: "It Takes a Tough Man to Make a Tender Chicken"

M&Ms: "Melt in Your Mouth, Not in Your Hands"

McDonald's: "You Deserve a Break Today"
Coke: "It's the Real Thing"
Prudential: "A Piece of the Rock"
Ford: "Have You Driven a Ford Lately?"
Michelin: "Because So Much Is Riding on Your Tires"

Creativity-Boosting Resources

Creativity in Business by Michael Ray and Rochelle
    Myers.
Writing the Natural Way by Gabrielle Lusser Rico,
    J. P. Tarcher, Inc. (distributed by Houghton
    Mifflin Company), 1983.
Whack on the Side of the Head by Roger von Oech,
    Warner Books, 1990.

There are also several exciting computer tools that can accelerate the idea-generating process and spark flashes of insight. They can help you meet challenges ranging from product-naming and headline generation to solving cash-flow problems and writing speeches. What this software won't do is solve the problem for you. What it will do is prod and prompt you into finding relationships and unexpected connections that may not have surfaced otherwise. One excellent idea-starter software program we recommend is *Ideafisher* (for PC or Macintosh). It's a thesaurus of ideas with more than 60,000 words, expressions, people, places, and things cross-referenced in more than 700,000 ways. Groupings of common traits and related concepts can spur new thinking to help you solve marketing challenges in original ways.

Twenty-Eight Ways to Make the News

No matter how you pitch the media, please remember the five F's: always be fast, fair, factual, frank, and friendly.

—Michael Levine

Publicity is one of the most cost-effective ways to get attention for your product, store, service, organization, idea, or cause. It requires little money to start off. But it can require some time to find the right medium for your product, create a good news release, send it out, and do the follow-up. As mentioned in the introduction to this book, 95 percent of the work in publicity is follow-up. Do that, and you will make the news.

How valuable is it to get news coverage? Here are just three common examples of what can happen when you make the news. Because much of my experience is in book publishing, many of my examples will be taken from that

121

source. But the basic principles will apply no matter what product, service, or cause you are promoting.

In 1989, *USA Today* featured Gregory Stock's *The Book of Questions* in a week-long series on the front page of the Life section. That same week, Workman Publishing had to go back to press for another printing of twenty-five thousand copies. The book went on to sell more than 550,000 copies in its first year. Plus, it sold to Book-of-the-Month Club, and negotiations were in the works for spin-offs of the book as a game and as a TV series.

When Abigail Van Buren mentioned Jim Trelease's *The Read-Aloud Handbook* in her "Dear Abby" column, sales of that book were boosted to more than 200,000 copies.

On November 21, 1991, Ann Landers told the readers of her syndicated advice column to go out and buy two copies of Dr. Isadore Rosenfield's *The Best Treatment.* By the end of that year, the book had shipped more than 285,000 copies, making it the fourteenth bestselling hardcover nonfiction title of that year.

So, how do you get your products, services, ideas, and groups featured in newspapers and magazines? Here are twenty-eight ways you can break into print. These are not listed in any particular order of priority.

Way 1: Work with Local Columnists

Every newspaper in the country, from the largest to the smallest, has at least one reporter whose duty it is to cover local people and events. Many of these columnists profile

When Abigail van Buren mentioned Jim Trelease's <u>The Read-Aloud Handbook</u> in her "Dear Abby" column, sales of that book were boosted to more than 200,000 copies.

products and services offered by local individuals and companies. These general interest columnists work hard to find interesting stories. Provide them with a good story and they will be happy to write about you. For example, I've seen books mentioned in Herb Caen's column in the *San Francisco Chronicle* (before he passed away) and in David Cataneo's "Hot Stove" sports column in the *Boston Herald*.

Way 2: Work with Specialized Columnists

Many local newspapers also have specialized columns such as Lee Svitak Dean's "Tidbits" column in the Taste section of the *Minneapolis Star Tribune*, or Pat Gardner's "Tender Years" column in the same publication. In one case, Dean featured *Uncle Gene's Bread Book for Kids* in his "Tidbits" column and even printed the price of the book and the address of the publisher—Happiness Press of Montgomery, New York.

Most newspapers have columnists who cover travel, gardening, careers, businesspeople, companies, housing, automobiles, food, restaurants, music, movies, and more. Take time for at least one week to read your newspaper every day and make note of those columnists who you think might be interested in what you are doing. Then put them into your contact database under "media."

If your newspaper doesn't have a columnist covering your area of interest, volunteer to be a freelance columnist. I've seen many large newspapers with, for example, real estate agents who wrote regular features in the Sunday

If your newspaper doesn't have a columnist covering your area of interest, volunteer to be a freelance columnist.

home section of their local newspaper. When it comes time for readers to contact someone to help sell their house, who do you think they will call?

Way 3: Work with Nationally Syndicated Columnists

There are fifteen hundred nationally syndicated columnists in the United States who write about everything from home decorating and repairs to advice about relationships, from real estate to entertainment, from business to child care. Almost all of them mention products, groups, services, and other resources at one time or another.

"Dr. Gott," a syndicated medical column by Dr. Peter Gott, recommended Jack Yetiv's self-published book, *Popular Nutritional Practices*, in answer to the following question from a reader: "I am confused about diet, weight loss, vitamin supplements, and the relation of diet to disease. Is there any up-to-date book on these subjects?" Yetiv's book would not have received this superb commendation if he had not sent a review copy to Dr. Gott.

Since Jane Brody featured *Kicking Your Stress Habits* in her column on personal health, Whole Person Press has sold more than 100,000 copies of the book by mail order.

In one of her columns, Ann Landers recommended Anna and Robert Leider's *Don't Miss Out*, as a solution to the college-financing blues. According to Longman Trade, the publisher of the book, more than 50,000 of Ann's readers responded to the notice. Note that Ann Landers is

Since Jane Brody featured <u>Kicking Your Stress Habits</u> in her column on personal health, Whole Person Press has sold more than 100,000 copies of the book by mail order.

syndicated in twelve hundred newspapers with a daily readership of ninety million people, many of whom follow her every word.

On September 19, 1990, Ann Landers featured a letter from a reader describing how she had cured her bladder incontinence by using exercises recommended in *Staying Dry*, a trade paperback published by Johns Hopkins University Press. Besides adding her own recommendation for the book, Ann printed the press's address in her column. As a result, they received more than 20,000 orders within three days and another 35,000 orders within the next month.

The Measure of Our Success became a bestseller after Marion Wright Edelman, the author, wrote a note to Ann Landers describing her activities with the Children's Defense Fund. Of course, she also enclosed a copy of her book. On July 19, 1992, Ann devoted her entire Sunday column to paraphrasing Edelman's lessons on life. When Beacon Press went back to press to print 40,000 more copies, they added a sticker noting Landers's recommendation.

To locate the major columnists, look in the syndicated columnist section of Ad-Lib Publication's *PR-ProfitCenter Database*. This informative section features the names, addresses, and phone numbers of seven hundred columnists. For details about the *PR-ProfitCenter Database*, call Ad-Lib at 800-669-0773.

Hint Why not have a friend from another part of the country write into a column recommending your product or service as a resource that helped him or her somehow?

Conduct a Survey

Most media love statistics. For example, USA Today runs a short visual statistic on its front page every day.

When Computer Associates announced that it was going to give away a million free copies of its Simply Money software, they included the results of a Gallup Poll that found that 77 percent of women say that they run the household finances, while 76 percent of men say they do. The results of this poll, of course, do not add up to 100 percent, as they should if both men and women were reporting accurately. Obviously many spouses are deluded as to who really runs the finances in their families. This discrepancy provided a good news hook that many media used to lead into the story of Computer Associates' giveaway.

Way 4: Self-Syndicate Your Own Column

You can syndicate your own column to newspapers, magazines, or newsletters. Much of the column's content could be taken from your consumer service literature or from questions your customers have asked you.

To promote her series of *Backyard Scientist* books, Jane Hoffman regularly sends out articles adapted from the books to a large number of home-schooling newsletters and other interested media. Many of these newsletters use her columns. Of course, each article ends with information on how the reader may order her books.

Jeffrey Lant, self-promoter extraordinaire and author of many books, writes a business self-help column that he syndicates to more than five hundred small-business and

You can syndicate your own column to newspapers, magazines, or newsletters.

opportunity publications. He claims his column has a readership of more than two million. In the past year, he has also begun syndicating his columns via the Internet, including e-mail distribution to key prospects.

Way 5: Set Up Your Own Press Syndicate

To establish your company as a source of information related to your specialties, establish a press syndicate. Such a syndicate does not need to be complicated. It could comprise a simple monthly mailing of news story ideas, feature articles, and other items.

Reebok, the athletic shoe manufacturer, sends out many of its background information releases under the auspices of the Reebok Aerobic Information Bureau. The Associated Press recently featured one of Reebok's releases about a study conducted by University of Southern California researchers that showed that exercising improves problem-solving abilities, concentration, and short-term memory. What a way to sell shoes!

Zondervan, a major publisher of religious books, has formed the Zondervan Press Syndicate, a free monthly feature service sent to interested newspaper and magazine editors. Each monthly mailing includes story ideas and camera-ready articles. Among the items they send regularly are feature articles, Q&A articles, word puzzles, book excerpts, cartoons, author columns, guest editorials, opinion articles, biographies, and special days-of-the-month material. Zondervan also mails out a monthly newsletter, *Producer's Report*, which features interview ideas for radio and TV producers. They also have formed the Zondervan Radio Network, which mails out free audiocassettes to 250 radio stations. The tapes feature various lengths of recorded material, from sixty-second news segments to twenty-seven-minute author interviews.

Way 6: Volunteer to Be an Expert

Let the media know that your owners, managers, or other key personnel are available as experts. Send them a bio and a background news release about your newest product or service. Later, follow up with copies of other articles that feature your expert (attach a "For Your Information" note to any follow-up copies). You might also publish a regular newsletter that you can send to all your media contacts. The key point is to keep your name continually in front of the media. Remember the 9/18 Relationship Marketing System!

Don't expect an immediate response. You won't always get one. Sooner or later, though, if you have matched your expertise to the media's needs, some will contact you to get more information. Every week, for example, *USA Today* features a special department, "Ask Money," where readers can ask questions that are, in turn, answered by leading experts around the country. Do you have any people who are qualified to answer such questions? If so, let the Money editors at *USA Today* know how to get in touch with them.

The *Minneapolis Star Tribune* has a regular column called "Fixit," which answers readers' questions about

Sooner or later, if you have matched your expertise to the media's needs, some will contact you to get more information.

consumer problems, from insurance to real estate. They often turn to outside experts to answer the questions from readers. Does your local newspaper have a similar column? If so, why aren't they calling you? Simple. You haven't yet established yourself as the expert to call. Do so today!

To keep its name in front of the media, *Playboy* magazine mailed out packs of Rolodex file cards to important media contacts. Each card in the pack was categorized by subject of expertise at the top and included the name of a *Playboy* editor or a regular contributor who could serve as an expert. Addresses and phone numbers were also listed. Experts were provided in the areas of art, sports, music, movies, photography, books, fashion, travel, and sex.

Way 7: Establish Yourself As a Prime Source

Here's an idea from State Farm Insurance. They prepared a short report, *A Reference Notebook of Insurance Sources*, which listed more than two hundred organizations that could provide information on insurance topics (the top insurance companies, trade associations, arson associations, and insurance research groups). They then placed ads in the major journalism publications (*Editor & Publisher, Quill, Columbia Journalism Review,* and *American Journalism Review*) inviting the media to send for a free copy of the report. Of course, State Farm was listed prominently as a resource in the report. But, more important, the fact that they were able to compile such a report clearly suggests that they were and continue to be the best source for information on insurance issues.

Way 8: Form Your Own Speakers Bureau

One way to make your authors or managers more available for speaking engagements with associations, groups, and businesses is to form a speakers bureau. You can fund the bureau with your commissions from paid speaking engagements. Matthew Bender, a legal publisher, formed a speakers bureau for its authors. Not only do they book their authors for seminars and conferences, but they also book them for media interviews.

Way 9: Sponsor a Poll

Conduct a survey related to one of your products or services. Then announce the results. Sometimes when you do this, you'll get featured twice: Once when you announce the survey and a second time when you announce the results. For example, Gallup did a poll for *Talk to Win*, a book by speech therapist Lillian Glass. The results of that poll were featured in many news stories.

Way 10: Sponsor a Contest

One effective way to get publicity is to sponsor a contest. You can even charge a small fee. How about a muffin-baking contest to promote a new food store? Or "your most romantic moment contest" to promote a new perfume. Or the best photo of the Grand Canyon for a new photography shop? Again, it's possible to get publicity both coming and going—when you announce the contest and when you announce the winner.

Several years ago, the *Wall Street Journal* publicized a contest sponsored by Delia's Restaurants. Delia's offered a chance to win a fully equipped Manhattan restaurant and one year's paid rent to the person with the best concept for a fantasy restaurant. The entry fee for the contest was $50. Delia's owners expected to get five thousand entries (that's $250,000 in entry fees) but reserved the right to

World Pizza Toss Contest

To publicize its new "tastes great, less fattening" mozzarella cheese, Lucille Farms decided to run a contest for the World Record Pizza Toss. To facilitate the contest, Lucille Farms persuaded New York City's Famous Original Ray's Pizza to host the event as a way of announcing the debut of its Garden DeLite Pizza. In addition to generating lots of publicity before and after the event, Sperling Green Associates, their PR firm, also arranged to have the United States' champion dough thrower, Carmine Carusone, compete as well as do the morning interviews before the contest. Nearly one thousand people showed up for a free sample of the low-fat pizza and to watch the contest. Ozzie Martinez, an out-of-work pizza man who was passing by the event, entered the contest and beat Carusone. Short news stories about the event were aired on CNN as well as major newscasts in New York, Philadelphia, Detroit, Atlanta, Los Angeles, Japan, and Spain. In a follow-up story, The New York Times rated the Garden DeLite Pizza as the pizza slice with the lowest fat available in Manhattan.

cancel the contest if that goal wasn't reached. What did Delia's get out of this contest? Well, they might have made some money on the contest fees, but they also got five thousand new ideas for trendy nightspots.

In its quarterly *Llewellyn New Times* newsletter, Llewellyn sponsored a book review contest. Readers were invited to submit a 750- to 1,000-word review of any Llewellyn title. Winners received a $20 gift certificate good toward any Llewellyn book, while Llewellyn received tons of great testimonials for their books.

Way 11: Solicit Suggestions for a New Product

USA Today often features solicitations for suggestions in the "Lifeline" column in its Life section. Recently, for example, it featured a request from Mifflin Lowe, author of *The Cheapskate's Handbook*, who sought the nation's biggest cheapskate. The winner received economy airfare to New York or Los Angeles. The runner-up won a $50 K-mart gift certificate.

In another column, CCC Publications requested contest entries for the most humorous answering machine messages for its forthcoming book, *No Hang-ups III.* They offered prizes of $1,000, $100, and $50, with fifty fourth-place prizes of $5. If CCC did its job right, every entry that was sent back was some sort of promotion about the first two books in the series.

Way 12: Get Listed in Community News

Most newspapers publish one or more events calendars. Some have separate calendars for sports, business, the arts, travel, and other important sections in the paper. Entertainment calendars are usually published on Friday, while business calendars are usually published on Monday. The *Minneapolis Star Tribune* has a separate events listings for senior citizens and another for families. Make sure your promotional events are listed in these calendars. Just send out a short news release (a short paragraph with the name of the event, time, date, place, and a short description is enough) to the calendar editor.

When you visit another city, arrange for an appearance at a local store, a speaking engagement, or some other public event. Then make sure your local contact gets the event listed in the Calendar or Events section of the local newspaper.

> **When you visit another city, arrange for an appearance at a local store, a speaking engagement, or some other public event.**

Way 13: Don't Forget the Wire Services

Many newspapers, which subscribe to one or more wire services, rely on the services to provide their readers with national news and features. It's common for a story that goes over the Associated Press wire to be picked up by two hundred or more newspapers. That's a quick way to get your story national coverage.

What is the best way to reach these services? Start by working with a reporter at your local metropolitan newspaper. Once the local paper publishes a story, especially if it's a good one, encourage the reporter or the editors to put the story on the wire. It's in their interest to have their stories go over the wire because it adds prestige to their work.

If your local newspaper doesn't do a story that appears on the wires, approach the local or regional bureaus for these news services. If you can't find their names in the yellow pages, call or write to the national headquarters:

> **Associated Press** (AP), 50 Rockefeller Plaza, New York, NY 10020-1666; 212-621-1500; fax: 212-621-7520. You can send story ideas to subject editors (sports, food, etc.).
>
> **United Press International** (UPI), 1510 H St. NW, Suite 600, Washington, DC 20005-2289; 202-898-8000; fax: 202-898-8057.
>
> **Reuters Information Services,** 1700 Broadway, New York, NY 10019-5945; 212-603-3300; fax: 212-603-3446.

Way 14: Submit Stories to Local News Bureaus

Major media often have bureaus in other cities. According to Allan Hall, technology editor at *Business Week*, you should submit a story twice to major magazines—one copy to the main editorial office and the other to the nearest bureau of the magazine. The chances are far greater that your local bureau will respond to your news release.

You should submit a story twice to major magazines—one copy to the main editorial office and the other to the nearest bureau of the magazine.

National News at a Local Level

When the Peanut Advisory Board conducted a national research study and discovered that most Americans identify peanut butter as a fun food to eat, they decided to capitalize on that perception. How? They convinced an entire town, Peanut, Pennsylvania (population 140), to stage a Peanut Butter Lovers' Festival to raise money for a local library and food bank. To publicize the event, they erected signs at the city limits saying, "Welcome to Peanut, Pennsylvania. We're Nuts About You!" In addition, they invited national media to attend and sample the world's largest peanut butter and jelly sandwich.

While only 950 people attended the actual event, one of those in attendance was the governor of Pennsylvania. Others in attendance included reporters from major media. Stories about the event were featured in Associated Press, UPI, CNN, CNBC, Washington Post, Wall Street Journal, and local TV affiliates in New York, Baltimore, Philadelphia, and St. Louis. The cost for the entire event? Only $7,000.

Why? Because it is their job to find local newsworthy events, people, and products.

Way 15: Track Down the Right Reporters

Sometimes you might have to contact four or five different editors at a newspaper before you find the one who would be most appropriate for you to tell about your product or service. It's worth the effort to track down the right editor or reporter. I know one publisher who had to send three review copies and make five calls to five different reporters at *USA Today* before he located a writer who was interested in reviewing his book/tape combos. But his persistence paid off—with a front-page feature in the Life section of *USA Today*.

When I sent a review copy of my trivia book, *Tinseltowns, U.S.A.*, to *USA Today*, I sent it to Tom Gliatto, then compiler of the "Lifeline" column, rather than the book editor. As a result, the book was featured in "Today's Tip-Off" at the top of the front page of the Life section.

Alan and Denise Fields, self-publishers of *Bridal Bargains: Secrets of Throwing a Fantastic Wedding on a Realistic Budget*, got a feature story about their book in the *Wall Street Journal* by contacting the magazine reporter. Why that reporter? Because the Fieldses had discovered that the bridal magazines were refusing advertisements from mail-order discount bridal companies. Of course, this policy created a controversy in the magazine industry, something the magazine reporter would be interested in probing. As a result of the *Wall Street Journal* article, the Fieldses got a call from *People* magazine—and a two-page spread in the magazine (with their toll-free number!).

Way 16: Track Down Freelance Writers

To get into newspapers, it often pays to track down a freelance writer who does a lot of work for those newspapers and who specializes in writing about subjects related to your book or product. Here's how one publisher located a freelance writer: "I called and asked who the family editor was. I wrote her, but I received no response. So I called again and this time asked for the assistant family editor. I

To get into newspapers, it often pays to track down a freelance writer.

wrote her as well. As a result of these two letters, one of them contacted a freelance writer living nearby. She wrote a superb article featuring our book."

Way 17: Submit to a Different Department

Again, sometimes one section of a newspaper or magazine will reject your news release while another will eagerly embrace it. It isn't always easy to tell which will like it. So, even though your news release was rejected by one department, it doesn't mean you can't resubmit the news to another department. For instance, if the "What's Up This Week" department of *Parade* magazine (which features forecasts of movies, records, and books) does not pay attention to your book, submit it to the "Bright Ideas to Make Life Better" department (which features new ideas on gardening, nutrition, health, parenting, and other how-to subjects).

Besides its feature stories and interviews, the in-flight magazine of American Airlines, *American Way*, also features short snippets on interesting travel trends and unusual sights in its "Sojourns" section—a perfect opening for travel-related products.

To promote David Pryce-Jones's book on improbable deaths, *You Can't Be Too Careful*, the publisher, Workman, sent copies of the book to the obituary writers at major newspapers. Along with the copy, they sent a little note suggesting that the writers review the book for their paper's book pages.

Even though your news release was rejected by one department, it doesn't mean you can't resubmit the news to another department.

Besides the regular departments, be on the lookout for seasonal features such as the perennial holiday gift section in many major magazines. Here is the story of the publisher of Down East Books, who happened to notice a listing about holiday gift features in my *Book Marketing Update* newsletter: "I noticed a blurb that *Playboy* might be looking for unusual gift ideas for their Christmas issue. We are currently publishing a very unusual book in a signed, limited edition called *Penobscot River Renaissance.* The possible marriage was just quirky enough that I thought it might work—it did! *Playboy* will review the book for their Christmas issue (with direct-response information, no less)."

> **Be on the lookout for seasonal features such as the perennial holiday gift section in many major magazines.**

Way 18: Write a Letter to the Editor

Or, better yet, submit a guest editorial to the newspaper. Write about something that really moves you. Write about your work, your ideas, your causes. Don't think that op-ed pages are worthless for publicity. They can be very effective. When Anthony Lewis praised *Under a Cruel Star: A Life in Prague 1941–1968* in the op-ed pages of the *New York Times*, the publisher had to go back to press for a second printing of three thousand copies.

Besides the letters-to-the-editor page, many newspapers and magazines also offer other opportunities for their readers to give them feedback. Here are a few of the ways that *USA Today* offers its readers an opportunity to give feedback: a toll-free number for readers to call in their letters to the editor or to give brief opinions, a toll-free number for the hearing impaired, an editorial fax number, and its "Voices from across the USA" editorial feature. If you'd like to give your opinion on a current topic of the day, send a clear, close-up photo of yourself along with your name, age, occupation, city, state, and day and nighttime phone numbers to: Voices, *USA Today*, 1000 Wilson Blvd., Arlington, VA 22229.

To encourage its readers to send news of successful direct-marketing campaigns, industry news, and other interesting items, *Direct* magazine prominently lists its Direct Hotline number as well as its fax number.

Readers of *Popular Mechanics* are invited to call any of eleven departmental editors via special Hotline numbers between 3:00 P.M. and 5:00 P.M. every Wednesday. Readers are encouraged to express opinions, ask questions, and offer story ideas.

PC World invites its readers to submit articles for its user columns, including "Star-Dot-Star," "Power Tips," and "The Upgrade Path."

Way 19: Offer Something Free

Many magazines have special departments that feature notices about new products, free reports, free samples, informational brochures, and other things that people can write away for. While it is almost impossible to get a magazine or newspaper to do a feature or review more than once on a new product or service, it is easy to get them to feature new free offers as often as you can come up with them. Plan to start a new promotional campaign at least

> While it is almost impossible to get a magazine or newspaper to do a feature or review more than once on a new product or service, it is easy to get them to feature new free offers as often as you can come up with them.

four times a year for each product or service you want to promote.

For example, a travel agent could offer a list of the ten most exciting places in Iowa (if they were promoting trips to Iowa). Two or three months later, the same agent could offer a report on holiday happenings in Iowa. Three months later, a report on how to plan your next vacation in Iowa. And three months later, a list of ten major historical sites in Iowa. And three months later . . . .

Family Circle magazine has a column, "Circle This," which consists of three pages of short items about new and unusual products. Some publishers have sold as many as twenty thousand books as a result of one mention in *Family Circle*.

Giveaways to Opinion Leaders

Besides offering free samples to consumers, be sure to send plenty of review copies to key opinion leaders in your field. When Farberware introduced its Millennium line of gourmet cookware for serious amateur chefs, it sent out dozens of samples to renowned professional chefs, cookbook authors, and cooking school operators. Given the cookware's real benefits—even distribution of heat and an indestructible finish—Farberware quickly received many testimonials. Peter Kump, head of the James Beard Cooking School, even agreed to appear in a promotional video for the Millennium line. As the line was introduced at retail, this video was played continuously in cookware departments of department stores. As a result of this giveaway promotion, Farberware was able to launch a major new product nationwide for less than $50,000 (about 10% of what most major nationwide product launches cost).

When readers write in
for your free offer, send
them your report or other
free gift plus your catalog
or other promotional
literature.

Freebies, a bimonthly newsletter that publishes all sorts of free offers, is especially interested in items for kids, crafts, home, auto, garden, and teachers. Send your items or news releases to: Freebies, 407 State St., P.O. Box 20283, Santa Barbara, CA 93120; 805-962-9135; fax: 805-962-1617.

When you make a free offer, make it something useful. And be sure it is related to your products or services. Then, when readers write in for your free offer, send them your report or other free gift plus your catalog or other promotional literature.

Way 20: Join a Press Association

Freelance writers and journalists often join press associations to mingle and network with other journalists. There are press associations for many interest groups, including a Catholic Press Association, Computer Press Association, and Garden Writer's Association. There are also writers associations for children's book writers, travel writers, sports writers, and so on. Seek out and join these associations to:

➥ Find professional writers who are qualified to write about your products—either in consumer media or for your press releases.

➥ Make connections with magazine and newspaper editors, radio and TV journalists, and freelance writers.

➡ Be the first to learn about editorial changes. Most press associations notify members of such changes long before others know.

Way 21: Use Co-Op Publicity Programs

To supplement your other promotional efforts, you might want to participate in a co-op publicity program or pay for a listing in one of the PR programs that are sent to editors and producers. Here are a few to get you started:

New Age Cooperative Mailings, First Editions, P.O. Box 2578, Sedona, AZ 86336; 602-282-9574; 800-777-4751; fax: 602-282-9730. First Editions organizes a number of cooperative mailing programs to New Age reviewers and bookstores.

The Women's Marketplace, 10125 Parkwood Dr., #8, P.O. Box 161775, Cupertino, CA 95016. This company offers co-op mailings to five hundred women's publications, five hundred women's bookstores, five hundred women's associations, three thousand libraries, and ten thousand women book buyers.

Radio-TV Interview Report, Bradley Communications, 135 E. Plumstead Ave., P.O. Box 1206, Lansdowne, PA 19050; 215-259-1070; fax: 215-284-3704. This bimonthly newsletter is sent to four thousand radio and TV producers.

Way 22: Distribute Releases via a PR Service

If you want to get your news out fast nationwide, you can work with one of the publicity services that distribute news releases electronically to newsrooms around the country. Here are a few such services:

PR Newswire, 1515 Broadway, New York, NY 10155; 212-832-9400; 800-832-5522; fax: 212-832-9406. They distribute news releases electronically to one thousand newsrooms across the country (both newspapers and broadcast).

North American Precis Syndicate, 201 E. 42nd Street, 32nd Floor, New York, NY 10017-5793; 212-867-9000. Besides news release distribution, this company can also handle multimedia releases and camera-ready releases.

You could also pay to have a news service send your story out by satellite feed to radio and TV producers. Here are a couple services that feed radio stations:

News/Broadcast Network, 149 Madison Ave., #804, New York, NY 10016; 212-889-0888; fax: 212-696-4611.

Jericho Promotions, 924 Broadway, 4th Floor, New York, NY 10010-6007; 212-260-3744; fax: 212-260-4168. Fifty percent of their stories feature books and authors. Their stories go to 1,100 subscribing radio stations.

Way 23: Distribute Camera-Ready Stories

Dr. Tony Hyman regularly sells over $100,000 in books every year by placing only three ads. How does he do it? He writes a short news story about his book, *Cash for Undiscovered Treasures*, and then distributes the story to seven thousand newspapers in camera-ready format designed for standard newspaper layouts. His stories are formatted and distributed by Metro Creative Graphics for about $1,000 per article.

Tony writes his own stories, but he makes sure they follow standard journalistic style so they read like a real news or feature story. His experience is that about two hundred newspapers pick up a story. And from that exposure, he sells some sixteen hundred copies of his $22.95 book. He grosses anywhere from $35,000 to $40,000 per story. To keep his book alive, Tony places three stories each year, with each story having a different slant. As a result, some newspapers have carried more than one story.

You could try to distribute your own camera-ready news stories, or you could use one of the services, such as Metro Creative Graphics, that regularly distribute such stories for a small fee. Both PR Newswire and North American Precis Syndicate distribute such stories. Here are a few other companies that offer this service:

> **Metro Creative Graphics,** 33 West 34th St., New York, NY 10001-3099; 212-947-5100; Fax: 212-714-9139. Besides sending out monthly mailings of camera-ready releases, this company also offers thematic sections such as Health and

Dr. Tony Hyman regularly sells over $100,000 in books every year by placing only three ads.

Fitness, Garden Time, Spring Home Improvement, and so on. Metro also offers a free clipping service for first-time participants of their services. **News USA,** 198 Van Buren St., #420, Herndon, VA 20170; 703-834-1818; fax: 703-834-1860. News USA will write, edit, typeset, print, and distribute a one-hundred-word feature in their monthly

Top Ten Lists

While David Letterman has popularized top ten lists among consumers, the print media has always had a strong interest in top ten lists. Here are a few top ten lists that have made big news:

- Fineman Associates, a San Francisco PR firm, has gained repeated national attention for its work as a result of its annual Top 10 Most Humiliating Public Relations Gaffes.

- In a recent e-mail news release, Hunting.Net sent out the Top 10 Reasons Why You Should Visit http://www.hunting.net. One of the reasons they listed was that the Hunting.Net site features the world's largest online collection of hunting videos.

- To promote his latest book, Cyberwriting, Joe Vitale worked with Paul Seaburn, a comedy writer for Jay Leno, to develop a humorous top ten list of reasons to read his book. Among those reasons were the fact that it's "cheaper than a night in the Lincoln bedroom and contains no ghosts of former presidents" and "rearrange the letters of each chapter title and find out what's really being stored in Area 51." Within hours of posting his top ten list to forty-nine friends, he noticed his message being spread across the Internet (confirming his theory that one thing that gets distributed via e-mail with little or no effort is humor).

tabloid of camera-ready articles that is sent to more than ten thousand newspapers. They provide usage reports and clippings as well.

Family Features Editorial Services, 8309 Melrose Dr., Shawnee Mission, KS 66214-3628; 913-888-3800; 800-443-2512. This company specializes in full-color thematic sections for the food and lifestyle pages of newspapers. They now also have a Web site at *http://www.culinary.net*.

Way 24: Get on <u>Oprah</u>

Always aim for the highest first. If you want to be on a national talk show, get on *The Oprah Winfrey Show*. If you want to get on a local TV talk show, go for the most watched one. It's not always easy, however, to book the top shows or top newspapers. As publicist Arielle Ford once said, "Here's how you get on *Oprah*. You call 213-385-0209." That's the Science of Mind prayer line. According to Ford, it's worked for some people. But here are a few more pointers on how to get on *Oprah*. Many of these pointers will also get results when working with other media.

Always aim for the highest first. If you want to be on a national talk show, get on <u>The Oprah Winfrey Show</u>.

Give the Producers a Show Idea

Don't say that you've got a great author or expert to interview. Present a show's producers with the entire show idea. What's the show's theme? Who else besides your expert should be on the show? Help them make the contacts for these other experts or case histories. Offer to share your resources to make the show happen. The more you do for them in creating an entire show, the more likely you are to get booked.

Provide a News Story

A new book being published is not a story; there are hundreds of new books published every day. The same holds true for new products and new services. Rarely do these make good stories. Discover the story behind your bland news release—and tell that story. How is your new product or service a story?

> Discover the story behind your bland news release— and tell that story.

Focus on People and Benefits

In your news release, pitch letter, and phone calls to media focus on the benefits of your product or service. How will it help people, especially the readers or viewers for the media you are approaching? Benefits, benefits, benefits—never features!

Quote People

Whenever possible quote users or your expert in your news releases. Why? Because quotes enliven any news story. Check it out for yourself. Read any news article and see how often the reporter quotes someone. Every news story uses quotes. It humanizes the story. For you, though, quotes offer one other incredible benefit: You can say anything you want in a quote. As long as the material is quoted, you can come out with a strong statement about your product or service and, often as not, the media will reprint it. Put the same words in your news release without quoting someone and not only won't the words be used, but there is a good chance your entire news release will be thrown out. Outrageous or strong statements should always be put in quotes.

> Every news story uses quotes. It humanizes the story.

Follow Up

For any important media contacts, always follow up your news releases with phone calls. Remember the importance of persistence and *follow up*. It is the most important key to success in publicity.

Make Repeated Contacts

If your first pitch to *Oprah* doesn't work, send another pitch, another show idea. Put the 9/18 Relationship Marketing System to work for you by contacting your most important media outlets at least once every two months. That's a minimum.

Way 25: Fax It

Most media now have fax machines and are equipped to receive news releases via fax. If you have a machine and access to media fax numbers, try sending some releases via fax. Don't, however, use faxes unless your story has real news value or immediacy. If there is one thing media people resent, it is having their fax machines (and their own time) tied up receiving puff stories.

Most fax machines can be set up to send the same fax to several hundred recipients whenever you want them sent. If you send them late at night, you can avoid the daytime fax rush, have your story on the editor's desk in the morning, and save money using the lowest late-night phone rates.

For a PR database that includes many fax numbers and e-mail addresses, get the *PR-ProfitCenter Database* from Open Horizons. Call 800-796-6130 for more information.

Way 26: E-Mail It

More and more media people have e-mail addresses and are receptive to receiving letters and product promotions via e-mail. Indeed, according to a new survey sponsored by the Columbia School of Journalism, a third of all editors go online daily (to do research, verify references, find sources, and check e-mail). Today, 29 percent of all journalists prefer to receive online information, while 50 percent prefer paper news releases. That's a dramatic shift from just two years ago, when only 17 percent were interested in online data.

To be safe (so they know it's a news release) and at the same time grab their interest, you should add a subject header with a good headline such as "Celebrate New Year's Every Month of the Year"—a headline John used right before New Year's Eve when promoting his book of holidays and anniversaries called *Celebrate Today!*

One great resource that provides e-mail addresses for thousands of media is the *U.S. All Media E-Mail Directory*.

Today, 29 percent of all journalists prefer to receive online information, while 50 percent prefer paper news releases.

Beware Headline Changes

How important is a headline? Judge for yourself: When <u>Sports Illustrated</u> began promoting its new <u>Sports Illustrated for Kids</u> via insert cards in the main magazine, it changed the headline on the card after it got some complaints. The original headline read: "Hey, Dad, kids love sports too!" The changed headline dropped the first two words to read: "Kids love sports too!" When they made the change, response to the card dropped by half. The lesson learned? The personalization of the "Hey, Dad!" was vital in appealing to the mostly male audience of <u>Sports Illustrated</u>. If you test any part of your news releases or direct mail letters, test your headlines. They are far more important than you might think.

Check out the Web site at *http://www.owt.com/dircon* for more information about the database directory. Also check out their short report *Ten Commandments for Sending E-Mail to the Media.*

Way 27: Teleconference

If you are holding a press conference or major media event, you might want to arrange a teleconference hookup with distant media. Several years ago, for example, Dow Jones-Irwin conducted a workshop based on its new book, *Service America,* that was beamed via satellite to 150 universities and corporate sites across the country. As a result of that initial push in publicity, the book sold fifty-five thousand copies in the first year.

Way 28: Put Your Information on the Internet

If you have a Web site, make sure you make your news releases and other promotions available on your site.

If you have a Web site, make sure you make your news releases and other promotions available on your site. Thousands of people will visit your site every year, especially if you are listed with all the major search engines. Check out John's Web site at *http://www. bookmarket. com.* More details on Internet publicity will be featured in the next chapter.

Bonus Points

As is always my practice, here are some bonus tips on how to get more publicity for your product, service, organization, idea, or cause. But, I repeat, the most important tip I can give you in doing publicity: Follow up. Follow up. Follow up.

Do Radio Phone Interviews

You can share your expertise on the air from the comfort of your home or office. To book these interviews, pay for an ad in *Radio-TV Interview Report* (Bradley Communications, 135 E. Plumstead Ave., P.O. Box 1206, Lansdowne, PA 19050-8206; 610-259-1070 or 800-989-1400; fax: 610-284-3704). You should, of course, also send press releases to major radio shows. Use *RTIR* as a supplement to your own efforts.

Get Listed in GuestFinder

GuestFinder is a site on the World Wide Web. Check it out at *http://www.guestfinder.com*. Many people get radio interviews from their paid listings on this Web site (a related site, ExpertFinder, features experts).

Send Out Unusual News Releases

As part of its promotion for Robert Shea's *All Things Are Lights*, Ballantine Books sent out a postcard release featuring the cover of the book. They also sent out custom-made candles tied into the book's title.

Sponsor a Contest

Radio shows and newspapers love contests. To promote *The Book of Inventions*, World Almanac sponsored a contest for the best invention by a reader of the book. The winner was then featured in the next edition of the book—and in another press release when the book was published.

Send Information to Alternative Media

Send press releases and news items to college newspapers, in-house publications, association newsletters, alumni magazines, and other off-the-beaten-track publications.

Try Unusual News Hooks

Learning Publications originally publicized its book *Joyful Learning* as a fun way to learn. Nothing new there.

Your Catalog As a News Release

To promote the publication of its annual <u>Brainstorms</u> holiday gift catalog, the Anatomical Chart Company sent a copy of the catalog along with a sticker pasted to its front cover that announced: "THIS IS MY PRESS RELEASE!"

The sticker went on to encourage radio and TV stations to call Marshall Cordell, president of <u>Brainstorms</u>, for an interview about zany gift ideas for the holidays. In addition, the sticker offered broadcast stations free on-air samples, free gift certificates, and free catalogs to any of their customers. Finally, it featured a list of the Top 10 Brainstorms Holiday Favorites, which included chocolate brain treats, alien embryo kits, toilet paper hats, giant bags of popcorn, and Eat Your Face gelatin molds.

But when they began publicizing the book as a way to help underachievers, the media jumped on the story. Now the book filled a definite need.

Make a Prediction

Forecast a trend. Newspapers love anything dramatic. Then, of course, when your prediction comes true, make sure they hear about that, too!

Forecast a trend. Newspapers love anything dramatic. Then, of course, when your prediction comes true, make sure they hear about that, too! That way you get two press mentions for the price of one!

Give Something Away

Free reports are best because they are inexpensive to produce, cheap and easy to mail, carry a high perceived value, and are inexhaustible. You should be able to write report after report in the subject area of your product, service, or cause. If you can't, change jobs. One of the wonderful things about free offers is that the newspaper or magazine has to print your address (so people can write away or call for the free report). Plus, because the report is free, the media see the news story as a service to their readers. You can charge a small fee for postage and handling ($1 to $3), so the promotion doesn't have to cost you a dime.

Give an Award

Make a donation for every sale. Announce a top ten list. Newspapers and radio shows love top ten lists. The annual Best Dressed List is a promotion. The Academy Awards are a promotion. And they always make the news.

Send Product Samples to Opinion Makers

When Warner Books published John Naisbitt's *Megatrends*, they sent copies of the book to the chief executives at the five hundred largest corporations in the country. As a result, they generated incredible word-of-mouth for the book, which went on to become a mega-bestseller.

Make It a Team Effort

Christopher Kuselias, CEO of Career TEAM in Hamden, Connecticut, requires every department head in his small job placement agency to produce one press release idea each month. The best ideas win a dinner for two or a pair

One of the wonderful things about free offers is that the newspaper or magazine has to print your address (so people can write away or call for the free report).

of movie tickets. The resulting publicity efforts yield at least two press mentions every month.

Focus on the Major Media

Always target the major media in your area. If you are a local business, make sure your metropolitan newspapers learn about you and your new services. If you are a new national business trying to reach amateur photographers, for example, make sure the magazines that reach those photographers do a story on your business. Put these major media in your 9/18 Relationship Marketing System database. And mail information to them at least once every two months. More often if you can.

Always Follow Up with Phone Calls

You won't always reach them. But even if you get lost in voice mail hell, leave a short message. That message should focus on one of the following: your unique selling proposition, a question, a statistic, or a very short anecdote—whatever you feel will most likely pique their interest. Then end with a brief offer to answer their questions. And leave your phone number.

Talk, Talk, Talk

When promoting his book *Swim with the Sharks without Being Eaten Alive*, Harvey Mackay talked to anyone who would listen. On one airplane flight, he noticed a passenger reading his book. Well, that got him started. He

If you are a new national business trying to reach amateur photographers, for example, make sure the magazines that reach those photographers do a story on your business.

introduced himself and then launched into a twenty-minute speech. He talked loudly enough that people could hear him in the back row. To explain the commotion, one of the flight attendants announced who Mackay was and also gave out the name of his book over the loudspeaker.

Do Five Promotions a Day

Make five phone calls. Write five letters. Send out five news releases. Or do a combination of things, but do at least five a day. Every day. Without fail. That's ten or fifteen minutes of work a day. But, if you do five promotions a day, you'll make at least a thousand contacts a year. If those contacts are legitimate targeted contacts, you'll get noticed—and you'll make the news. Guaranteed!

Master Internet Marketing

4

The future belongs to those who see possibilities before they become obvious.

—Theodore Levitt

In the past five years, a real revolution has taken place, one that will offer small businesses greater reach and greater impact than any other marketing innovation of the past century: the Internet and, more specifically, the World Wide Web. It is still in its infancy, but the opportunities it offers small businesses and professionals are limited only by your imagination. That's why we're devoting an entire chapter to marketing via the Net.

While it may seem that the Internet has been hyped to death, the reality is that it truly does offer small businesses an economical way to reach customers around the world with offers that can change by the minute. Never before has there been such a low-cost, flexible,

157

wide-reaching means for testing and carrying out all sorts of promotions. Let's look at some of the numbers:

More than 50 million people are now using the Internet worldwide. By the time you read this, that number could easily have doubled. By the year 2000, conservative estimates suggest that 150 million people will be on the Net. As of this writing, according to Jupiter Communications, more than 4.1 million children surf the Web.

More e-mails (messages sent via the Internet) are being sent out today than "snail mail" (letters sent via the post office). Forty percent of business cards now feature an e-mail address.

According to a survey conducted early in 1997 by ActivMedia, Net-generated sales were expected to reach $13 billion in 1997.

According to a 1997 CommerceNet/Nielson survey, 73 percent of Internet users have used it for shopping during the past month. By 2000, 46 million American consumers will spend an average of $350 per year shopping on the Net.

Two hundred and seventy-five million dollars was spent on advertising via the Net in 1996. According to Michael Tchong of CyberAtlas, Internet advertising revenues are expected to reach $5 billion by the year 2000. Ad revenues for April 1997 tripled those for April 1996 (according to Simba's *Electronic Advertising & Marketplace Report*).

According to a 1996 ActivMedia survey, 31 percent of all commercial Web sites were profitable (with at least another 10 percent expected to be profitable by the end of 1997). In an informal survey at the 1996 BookExpo

The reality is that the Internet truly does offer small businesses an economical way to reach customers around the world with offers that can change by the minute.

America convention, 50 percent of the booksellers on the Web said their sites were making money. Of course, the converse (that 50 percent were not making money) should alert you to be cautious when expanding onto the Web.

Twenty percent of retailers now offer online shopping. In 1996, only 11 percent did. In 1995, only 5 percent. An additional 37 percent of retailers, according to a CSC survey, plan to offer online shopping in the near future.

According to a recent survey conducted by Netsmart Research, eight out of ten Internet users routinely use the Web to research products and services (and report that the Web helps them make better buying decisions). Forty-six percent go on to buy the product at retail.

Eighty-one percent of the members of the Direct Marketing Association currently use the Internet in some way. Another 16 percent are considering its use. Of the 81 percent who currently use the Internet, 49 percent use it primarily for sales.

According to a recent survey conducted by Netsmart Research, eight out of ten Internet users routinely use the Web to research products and services.

Who's Making Money on the Net?

The Internet is not all hype. Companies are making money and sales on the Net right now. Here are a few examples:

By February 1997, after only four months in business, Microsoft's Internet travel service, Expedia, was selling $1 million worth of airline tickets every week. Online travel sales, according to Jupiter Communications, are expected to reach $4.7 billion by 2000 and $8.9 billion by 2002.

Netscape, number one in Internet ad sales, made $27.7 million in ad sales for its Web site in 1996. Netscape expected more than $60 million in ad sales for 1997. CNN, the Cable News Network, had Web ad revenues of $1.8 million in April 1997. *USA Today*'s Web site had ad sales of $825,000 during that same month.

Several years ago, a small retail store in Pasadena, California, set up a site featuring hot sauces (*http://www.hothothot.com*). It now offers more than 150 such sauces to a worldwide audience of spicy food aficionados. As a result, it has attracted dozens of online competitors, but it was first and still gets most of the publicity.

The brokerage firm of Charles Schwab & Co. has more than 700,000 active online accounts with customer assets of $50 billion.

Auto-by-Tel, an Internet car sales broker, has had a hand in selling more than $2 billion worth of automobiles. It is responsible for more sales in one month than the largest traditional car dealers make in an entire year.

J&D Resources, a temporary employment and permanent placement service, set up a Web site about two years ago. The company designed its own site and spent about $900 to set it up, register the domain name, and include the site in about two hundred search engines and Web indexes. Monthly costs to maintain the site include $50 for the host service and $100 for advertising on career-related sites. The company's Web site has increased its annual revenues by 5 percent, or about $100,000.

CDNow, an online retailer of music CDs and videos, had sales of $6 million in 1996 and made an operating profit of 18 percent.

Sales Predictions

The following stats are taken from a free weekly e-mail newsletter, Internet Surveys, published by NUA Limited. To subscribe to Internet Surveys, send e-mail to: surveys request@nua.ie with the following message in the text: subscribe.

Anderson Consulting predicts that the online grocery shopping market will grow to $60 billion in the next 10 years.

Jupiter predicts that online CD sales will more than double this year to $47 million, up from $19 million in 1996, and that by 2002, online sales of pre-recorded music will total $1.6 billion, or 7.5 percent of the overall music market.

In 1996, Gateway 2000 had $40 million in online computer sales.

Dell Computer reports that it has been selling $1 million worth of computers every day. Its Web site allows customers to design their own PCs, generate price quotes, order or lease products, and track the status of their orders.

In December 1996, eighty thousand flower and gift orders were placed on the Web site of 1-800-FLOWERS, accounting for $4 million in sales. Web sales accounted for 10 percent of the company's holiday sales in 1996.

According to *The New York Times*, Cisco Systems currently sells more than $5 million in systems every day. Within a year, the company expects to be selling $2 billion in systems per year. As the company notes, "Business-to-business commerce is the killer application of the Internet." In addition to sales, Cisco has also moved its credit checking, basic technical support, routine customer support, and production scheduling to the Internet.

All One Tribe, a small drum shop in Taos, New Mexico, set up a Web site in 1995. Having unsuccessfully tried ads in *New Age Journal* and other publications to expand drum sales beyond local visitors, the store now reaches a worldwide audience via the Net. Start-up costs for the All One Tribe Web site were about $350. Monthly costs include $50 for Web space and $200 for promotion. As a result, they've made sales as far away as Australia and Germany.

Floaty Industries, sellers of floaty pens, received 200,000 hits on its Web site in March 1997. Four thousand people registered at the site, and two hundred people placed orders. With an average online order of about $20, the site generates $4,000 in orders per month.

Rent.Net, an apartment hunter's resource, is a Web-only company that funds itself by payments from apartment owners and Web advertisers. Begun by two friends, it now has forty-five employees and listings in twelve hundred U.S. cities. They spend tens of thousands of dollars in Web advertising every month to promote their site and still make money. The Internet provides Rent.Net with its one major edge over printed housing guides: They can implement content changes the very same day.

United Parcel Service has recently formed a partnership with several leading search engines, including Lycos, Infoseek, and Yahoo, to allow customers to track their UPS shipments from the search engine sites. UPS expects to double its Net tracking activity, with more than 340,000 requests from those sites alone.

General Electric will source $1 billion worth of goods from more than fourteen hundred suppliers this year via its Web-based Trading Process Network.

FreeShop Online, an Internet free-sampling site (*http: //www.freeshop.com*), recently processed its two millionth order since opening shop in December 1994. Among other offers, FreeShop has given away forty thousand rolls of film from Seattle Filmworks and twenty thousand trial subscriptions to the *Wall Street Journal.*

Why You Need to Set Up Your Own Web Site

To sell a product or market your service on the Internet you must set up a Web site (a collection of Web pages that fit together as a unit). Such a site gives you a worldwide twenty-four-hour sales and marketing presence. In the

Get to Know the Web

Some of the following pages will introduce words and concepts that are exclusive to the Web. We'll try to define them as we go along, but you may not really understand them until you actually spend a little time browsing the Web yourself. If you intend to market your products or services on the Net, you need to learn the basics by using the Web regularly. Many of the jobs of creating, maintaining, and marketing a Web site can be farmed out, but if you don't understand the way the Web works, you won't be able to adequately communicate your needs to those who will do the designing and marketing of your site.

Also, since the Web has been changing very quickly, we can't guarantee that all the information we provide in the rest of this chapter will still be current when you read this book. To help you out, we will provide updated information on my Web site, Book Market, at http://www.bookmarket.com.

beginning of the commercialization of the Web, the most successful sites were selling advertising space. In the near future, however, most sites will be built on a direct-marketing model where the focus is on selling products or services, generating sales leads, finding partners, cutting distribution costs, and providing customer service.

First, decide on a primary business model for your site. Will you rely on advertising sales, product sales, subscriptions, or something else to make money? According to an April 1997 survey conducted by *Net Profit Online* magazine, at present 46 percent of commercial Web sites rely on advertising, 39 percent rely on product sales, and 2 percent rely on subscriptions. The remaining 13 percent have some other business model.

The main Web strategy of large corporate members of the Association of National Advertisers is to offer product and service information. Other priorities include corporate image, advertising, and customer service. Direct sales ranks sixth among their priorities for their Web sites. Small businesses, however, can't afford such strategies. Sales must be first because the site must pay for itself.

Here are a few ways you can market your products and services on the Net. Use this list to help you develop a focus for your site.

➡ Sell your product direct to the consumer. Rodale Press has set up many Web sites to promote its various books and magazines. Rodale has discovered that it costs about $20,000 to launch a Web site that duplicates a direct-mail package that costs about $75,000 to design and test. Their

> First, decide on a primary business model for your site. Will you rely on advertising sales, product sales, subscriptions, or something else to make money?

Web sites are currently selling about three thousand books a month.

➡ Send your customers to your distributor or retail outlets to buy your product.

➡ Expose your product or service to millions worldwide, or target a local audience by participating in one of the many city-specific sites now forming on the Net (most sponsored by local newspapers).

➡ Sponsor your own online discussion or support group for your product.

➡ Sell advertising on your pages to other companies. Currently, only about a thousand sites (out of millions) carry any significant amount of advertising.

➡ Create exclusive content on your site that people can access only if they subscribe to the additional service or pay-per-view (pay each time they use that part of your site). Hoover's Inc., publishers of proprietary information on eleven thousand U.S. companies, generates 60 percent of its online revenues from advertising and 40 percent from subscriptions. "We're big believers in offering free, high-quality information supported by advertising, with deeper, more robust information available on a subscription basis," says their CEO, Patrick Spain. "Neither revenue model," he adds, "would be enough by itself, but together, we're profitable." Hoover's charges $10 per month for unlimited access and already has several thousand subscribers.

➡ Provide technical and/or customer support via your Web site. For example, FedEx allows customers to track their shipments directly.

Create exclusive content on your site that people can access only if they subscribe to the additional service or pay-per-view.

Customers get the information they're looking for more quickly than through a phone call, and FedEx saves $3 on not answering the phone and replying to the customer in person.

➡ Create customer loyalty programs that keep customers coming back to you.

➡ Carry out publicity campaigns via the Net. The producers of many radio and television shows (including *The Oprah Winfrey Show*) are using the Net to find guests.

➡ Build mailing lists (or e-mail lists) of customers to whom you can send information about new products or services. There are a number of ways to capture the names, addresses, phone numbers, and e-mail addresses of people who visit your site, including guest books and e-mail newsletters. We'll discuss those later.

➡ Post your catalog on your Web site.

➡ Or allow people to request your catalog. Soda Creek Press, publishers of the *Mysteries by Mail* and *Manderley* catalogs, have experienced a 4 percent sales conversion rate on catalogs requested on their Web site as opposed to a less than 2 percent sales conversion rate from their direct-mail campaigns.

➡ Survey your customers via a survey page on your site or by e-mail.

➡ Set up a registry service for weddings, birthdays, or holiday giving.

➡ Set up a classified ad section on your site. One woman in Italy spotted a Dodge Viper for sale in the *Chicago Tribune*'s online classified ad section.

Sites for Professional Services

The Internet is shaping up to be one of the best tools for marketing professional services, such as lawyers, accountants, and consultants. Three years ago, Gregory Siskind was a Nashville attorney with a dream of becoming an immigration lawyer. Today, with a Web site that features one thousand pages of government forms and other details on immigration law (http://www.visalaw.com), his practice has expanded to six states. Two-thirds of his business comes from his Web site and monthly e-mail newsletter (with 10,000 subscribers).

Lewis Rose, another attorney, has added 30 new clients and $300,000 in additional revenue over 16 months—all as a result of his firm's Web site (http://www.arentfox.com). As he noted, "The Internet has been the most cost-effective way of getting my name out there."

The key to success for professional Web sites is to avoid advertising and include plenty of useful content. Here, according to a recent Business Marketing article, are a few other pointers for making your professional Web site work:

- SHOW, DON'T TELL. Demonstrate your expertise by providing plenty of good content and lots of free reports.
- KEEP YOUR SITE SIMPLE. Don't load up on fancy graphics, animation, videos, or other gimmicks. Load up on content instead.
- TARGET YOUR AUDIENCE. Think of what your potential customers would like to see. Then provide it. Keep your site focused on the needs of your audience.
- RESPOND QUICKLY. Internet users expect fast responses. Try to answer any questions from Web site visitors within 24 hours.
- MAKE IT EASY TO REACH YOU. Display your e-mail connection prominently so it's easy for people to reach you.
- GET THE WORD OUT. As with any Web site, you have to promote it by posting to newsgroups, trading links, getting listed in the search engines, and doing off-Web traditional marketing and promotion.

- Provide related background information that draws potential customers to your site. Establish your site as the place to come for information in your area of expertise.
- Provide updates. This service is especially useful if you sell books, software, or other information. Many software companies allow buyers to download updates and fixes for free for the first year and for a small fee afterwards.
- Join associate sales programs or referral programs to generate income for your site.
- Upload your annual report. IBM has done that now for two years in a row. Among other things, their online annual report allows investors to compare five years of IBM's performance on more than a dozen points, including net earnings and total revenue.

Set Up Your Own Web Site

The most important thing is to create a Web site that has its own distinct identity. That means that you should get your own domain name rather than house your service solely among the pages of an online shopping mall or on-line service. A domain name makes it easy for people to find you. For example, John's domain name for his book marketing site is bookmarket.com.

Registering your own domain name protects your trademark or company name. Otherwise, another company or similar product could take a domain name that others would think of as yours. For example, in the early

Registering your own domain name protects your trademark or company name. Otherwise, another company or similar product could take a domain name that others would think of as yours.

days of the Web, a freelance writer registered the domain name mcdonalds.com. It cost McDonald's a lot of time and money to get that domain name back for its own use.

Most people, when searching for a company or product, first try to search for the company by typing in www.yourcompany.com or www.yourproduct.com. Having your own domain name says that you are big enough to merit your own domain. It allows you to stand out much more than you would in a mall. Your own domain name allows you to create a short, memorable name that people will remember, is easy for you to repeat over the phone, and will fit on your business card.

With your own domain name, you can switch service providers and not worry about your customers not being able to find you. For small businesses, it doesn't pay to host your own site on an in-house computer (since the cost of hardware, software, and support is high). Instead, select a host service that can provide you with a secure and fast connection to the Web as well as other services you might require to make your site operational. Don't try to save money by using a low-powered Web host.

Domain names can be worth a lot of money. Early in 1997, Mecklermedia paid The Internet Company more than $100,000 for the internet.com domain name. Several months later, a Texas company bought the name business.com for $150,000—the highest price yet paid for an Internet domain name.

To reserve your domain name, contact InterNIC Registration Services by calling 703-742-4777 or by e-mailing: *hostmaster@internic.net*. The cost of setting up a domain name is $100 for the first year and $50 per year thereafter. Note that new domain names using extensions

> Having your own domain name says that you are big enough to merit your own domain. It allows you to stand out much more than you would in a mall.

other than .com (such as .firm, .store, .Web, and .info) will probably be available by the time you read this. What's more, they may cost less since there is a good chance that more than one firm will be allowed to process and assign these additional domain names. Competition should drive the price down.

To have your site hosted on a Web server, contact the company that provides your current Internet service. Most companies also provide Web page–hosting services. For example, EarthLink Network, one of the largest Internet service providers (ISPs), also provides Web hosting with your unique domain name for as little as a $279 setup fee plus monthly fees.

Here are a few other low-cost hosting services that you might want to check out: OneHost (*http://www.onehost.com*), ValueWeb (888-934-6788), and HiWay Technologies (561-989-8574; 800-339-4929; *http://www.hiway.net*). HiWay currently hosts twenty thousand domains for only $24.95 per month per domain. ValueWeb and One-Host offer plans for as low as $19.95 per month. Another company, Infoboard (800-514-2297; *http://www.ifoboard.com*), provides complete hosting and setup services, including up to 1 gigabyte (100 megabytes) of space for a $150 setup fee and $150 per month.

Design Your Web Site

Once you have a domain name registered and have arranged for a hosting service, you can start designing your Web site. Read on for some tips on how to go about designing an effective site.

Games, Games, Games

Games and contests are some of the best tools you can use to get consumers to come back to your site again and again. According to Michael Simon, president of E-Pub Inc., "Gaming is shaping up to possibly become the killer app that the Web has been seeking. Games are proven tools for building traffic, usage, and an online community."

When building your Web site, start slowly. Keep it simple in the beginning. You can take time to build and make revisions.

Take a look at other Web sites. Check out which ones you like the best. What features make the site easy for you to use? What content appeals to you? What designs do you like best? Select the best elements of your favorite sites and incorporate those features into your site.

You can create the site yourself using software such as Claris *HomePage* (the software I used to create bookmarket.com), or you can hire someone who has experience designing and creating such sites. Before you hire someone, check out the sites he or she has already created. Make sure the designer can handle the kinds of features you want to incorporate into your site. While Claris *HomePage* and other easy-to-use programs allow you to design a site, they don't yet enable you to create shopping carts, database searches, and other features you might want. For those advanced features, you will have to work with a Web site creator.

Start slowly. Keep it simple in the beginning. You can take time to build and make revisions. There is no rush to have everything perfect from the start. Start with the basics. You can add shopping carts and database wizards later.

Place an emphasis on content. Provide good, usable content that is updated on a regular basis. Internet users are very content-oriented. If you don't know how to create useful content, you can hire writers to provide content appropriate for your site or license rights to existing content (from books, magazine articles, newsletter tips, associations, government agencies, etc.). You can also pick up free content from the following two sites: Article Resource Association (*http://www.aracopy.com*) and the World Wide Information Outlet (*http://certificate.net/wwio*).

Make it easy for people to get around your site. Especially make it easy for them to get to your home page and site map (if you have one). That's easy to do: Just provide links back to your home page on every page in your site.

Avoid using too many graphical elements, animation, sound, or other elements that make your Web pages download slowly. Remember that many users still have slow modems or service providers. Keep your site simple in the beginning.

Maintain your image. Don't try to create an image that is different from your real-world image. Use the Web as an adjunct to your other marketing and promotion.

What causes people to come back for return visits? According to IntelliQuest, 56 percent return to sites they find entertaining. Other attractive attributes include: 54 percent like attention-grabbing sites, 53 percent extremely useful content, 45 percent information tailored to their needs, 39 percent thought-provoking content, 39 percent visually appealing sites, 38 percent imaginative sites, and 36 percent highly interactive sites.

Avoid using too many graphical elements, animation, sound, or other elements that make your Web pages download slowly.

Provide people with a way to register with your site to receive updates or further information from your company (a guest book).

What do Web site designers recommend? Among other page design elements, they suggest: Make everything as big as possible. Don't use a lot of text. Use lots of white space and margins. Whenever possible, don't make people scroll.

Provide people with a way to register with your site to receive updates or further information from your company (a guest book). You can set up an e-mail newsletter for this purpose. Most hosting services or Internet service providers can set up and maintain an automatic sign-up system for the newsletter that allows users to sign up without your intervention and allows you to send out a newsletter or sales message to all people on the list with one e-mail message.

Make your Web site friendlier to sight-impaired readers. As a start, offer a text-only version. For more info on making your Web site more accessible to the sight-impaired, check out the Trace R&D Center at *http://www.trace.wisc.edu/world/Web/index.html*. Also, Gene Barnett of the Eel River Redwoods Hostel has set up a superb tip page for Designing Speech-Friendly Web Pages for the Blind. Check his page out at *http://northcoast.com/~ebarnett/browsers/speech-friendly.html*.

If you have a large potential market overseas, design your site with certain pages that are written in the language or languages of your target audience. At the minimum, make your offer, information page, and order form available in other languages. There are some Web resources that make it easier for you to translate certain pages into other languages. You can find these resources by using one of the Internet search engines (described later in this chapter). If you do set up pages in other languages, be sure to register your site with foreign-language search engines.

You can set up your Web site so people can enter from any of a number of pages on your site. For instance, you could have a home page, where most people would enter. But you might also have a bookstore, library, events listing, directory, chat area, or detailed article that would attract many first-time viewers who would go on to view other parts of your site. In fact, if you have a site that could attract a number of different special-interest groups, you might set up entrance pages for each group. For instance, bookmarket.com has separate entrance pages for writers, publishers, publicists, general marketers, Internet marketers, and the general public. That way, I can set up and publicize home pages that make my site look as if it addresses the special needs of each of these audiences.

If you have a local retail store, put a map on your site that details the location of your store. Your site provider may already have the capability to add map pages to your site. There is also one site that allows you to link your address to a mapping service (*http://www.vicinity.com*).

Be sure to give your home page a title that will attract the most viewers to your Web site. Many search engines use the title as one criterion for selecting sites to include in their site index. The first paragraph of text after your title is also often used by search engines to rank listings, so be sure the first paragraph contains key words about the contents of your site.

To increase your rankings in some search engines, you can also add metatags at the top of your HTML page (HTML, hypertext markup language, is the code language

Be sure to give your home page a title that will attract the most viewers to your Web site.

for designing Web pages). Here's an example of a metatag: <meta tags="key words" Content="book, books, publisher, publishers, publishing, marketing, sales, advertising, publicity, promotion, writing, authors, directory">. This is one of the metatags on my home page. It tells search engines some of the key words that a person might use to search for the information on my bookmarket.com site. These metatags do not show up on any home page viewed by a Web browser but can be looked at if you open the source code in your browser. Ask someone familiar with browsing the Web to help you with this if you don't know how.

Somewhere on your site, include a links page to other relevant sites. Also add links to relevant sites wherever appropriate on your site. Web surfers love sites with lots of links and will return to your site often just to make use of your links. Also some of the search engines rank a Web site by the number of links it has to other sites (and the number of other sites that have links to it).

If you plan to take orders on your Web site, be sure to list that you accept credit cards since that is the most common way people pay for things bought online. Plus it makes your product more accessible to people overseas. Floaty Industries, which sells special floaty pens, found that orders increased in number and size after it began accepting credit cards.

On your home page, include the words "Bookmark this page." This tells people to make your site a bookmark, or favorite, that they will come back to again and again.

Provide useful information on your site. When Pfizer wanted to promote Zyrtec, a new allergy medication, they designed an interactive house on the Web where allergy

Web surfers love sites with lots of links and will return to your site often just to make use of your links.

sufferers could find out all the latest information on how to allergy-proof each room of their homes, including how to clean drapes, bathe pets, and use air filters. In addition, Pfizer worked with the National Allergy Bureau to include updates on pollen counts for various parts of the country. Pfizer even created a separate domain name for this part of its site. Now allergy doctors are giving out *http://www.allergyinfo.com* to all their patients! Here are a few other sites you might want to check out to see what they do to attract visitors:

Provide useful information on your site.

Anti-Telemarketer Source (*http://www.izzy.net/~vnestico/t-market.html*)

Celebrate Today (*http://www.bookmarket.com/celebrate.html*)

Computer Virus Myths (*http://www.kumite.com/ myths*)

Jolt Cola (*http://www.joltcola.com/main.html*)

Poet's Corner (*http://www.lexmark.com/data/poem/poem.html*)

Research Paper (*http://www.researchpaper.com/index.html*)

Tide Clothesline Stain Detective (*http://www.clothesline.com/stainDet/index.html*)

Whale Watcher Expert System (*http://vvv.com/ai/demos/whale.html*)

Once you have your site up and running, surf over to *http://www.sitegrade.com* to have volunteers review and grade your site for ease of use and content.

Also go to Dr. HTML (*http://www2.imagiware.com/RxHTML*) for a free testing service that will test a single

URL (Web address) and report back to you on spelling, form structure, link verification, and other aspects of your Web page. Your entire site can be checked for a fee.

Market Your Web Site

With more than one million Web sites and eighty million HTML pages in existence, it takes something extra to stand out. Given that most users visit about twenty Web pages per day, it would take one person several lifetimes to visit just the home page of every site and many, many lifetimes to visit every page. Currently, one thousand sites account for half the traffic on the Web. How, then, can you make your site one of those top one thousand?

The old rule, "If you build a better mousetrap, people will beat a path to your door," simply does not apply to Web sites. Once you build your Web site, you must market it. Now that might seem rather silly since we have been recommending that you build a Web site as a way to market your products or services—and now we're telling you that you will have to market your new marketing tool. So why go through all the trouble of setting up a Web site? Three reasons:

1. To keep up with the Joneses (your competition will have a site soon if they don't already, and you need to keep up with them or lose some business to them).

2. A Web site will allow you to reach an audience you are not currently reaching through any other means, especially a worldwide audience.

The old rule, "If you build a better mousetrap, people will beat a path to your door," simply does not apply to Web sites.

3. Much of the marketing for your Web site must occur at the beginning. Once you have done the basics, your ongoing Web marketing doesn't have to require a lot of extra time.

Make Your E-mail and Web Addresses Known

Add your e-mail address and Web site URL to your business card, letterhead, catalogs, brochures, advertisements, packaging, and other marketing materials. Your URL (uniform resource locator) is your Web site address. Some underwear companies, including Big Dogs and Joe Boxer, even print their URLs on the waistbands of their boxer shorts. Nowadays, you would not allow any marketing material to go out without your fax number on it. Within five years, the same will be true for e-mail addresses and Web site URLs, so why not start now?

Create an E-mail Signature

Add a signature to your outgoing e-mail messages and newsgroup postings. One of the best ways to get people to your site is to feature its address in your e-mail signature. Keep your signature less than six lines. Be sure to include your name, e-mail address, Web site URL, and the names or features of one or two of your products or services. I'll use my e-mail signature as an example:

```
=======================================
```

John Kremer, editor, Book Marketing Update newsletter and author of *1001 Ways to Market Your Books* and *Celebrate Today!*

Nowadays, you would not allow any marketing material to go out without your fax number on it. Within five years, the same will be true for e-mail addresses and Web site URLs, so why not start now?

Open Horizons, P.O. Box 205, Fairfield, IA 52556; 800-796-6130

Subscribe to his free Marketing Tip of the Week by visiting his Web site.

E-mail: JohnKremer@bookmarket.com | Web: *http://www.bookmarket.com*

==

Submit Your Site to the Major Search Engines

Web search engines are large indexes where most Web surfers go when they want to research a new topic. Search engines are the primary way that most people will find out about your site. Here are seven big search engines where you should have your site listed.

> AltaVista (*http://www.altavista.digital.com*)— Features more than twenty-one million sites! AltaVista also offers a section called Live Topics, where people can filter search results to find out which sites are relevant to their needs.
>
> Excite (*http://www.excite.com*)
>
> HotBot (*http://www.hotbot.com*)—This site does not enter into frame sites.
>
> Infoseek (*http://www.infoseek.com*)
>
> Lycos (*http://www.lycos.com*)
>
> OpenText (*http://index.opentext.net*)—Click on the "Add Your URL" link. Note that you can add links not only to your home page but also to other special-interest entrance pages on your site.
>
> Webcrawler (*http://Webcrawler.com*)

Since search engines can list hundreds of thousands of pages in response to one query, it is important that you do everything possible to increase your ranking.

Search Engine Listings

In July 1997, NetGambit, developer of the PositionAgent search engine, completed the first study of the importance of top search engines in helping to generate Web traffic. Of the fifteen hundred Web site owners polled, 48 percent depend on search engine listings for the majority of their traffic (averaging 26,000 visitors per month). Twenty percent of all Web traffic is generated by the top search engines and directories.

Web search engines take from a few minutes to four weeks to list your site's home page and up to six additional weeks to list the rest of the pages on your site. In the section on designing your Web site, we listed some of the design elements you can use to increase your rank in these search engine listings (such as titles, metatags, links, key words at the beginning of your site, and the frequency of changes at your site). Since search engines can list hundreds of thousands of pages in response to one query, it is important that you do everything possible to increase your ranking (few people will look at pages beyond the first hundred listed in their query results). For more information on designing your Web page for search engines, check out *http://searchenginewatch.com.*

A month after you make your submissions to these search engines, you might want to review how your site ranks by the key words people might use to search for your site. To do this, go to Rank This! (*http://www.rank this.com*). This site allows you to check all seven major search engines plus Yahoo (a Web site index) to see how you rank. It goes to each engine one at a time and tells you if your site is listed in the top two hundred positions. It also lists those sites that made the top ten listings. In just a few minutes, not only will you know how your site ranks, but you will also have gathered a list of pages that are getting better rankings. Check out those pages and try to figure out why they are getting higher rankings. Then change your page accordingly.

There are also many super search engines that allow you to search two or more major search engines at once. You do not need to submit your site to these super search engines because they derive all of their content from the other search engines. Here are the addresses of a few of the super search engines:

Ask Jeeves (*http://www.askjeeves.com*)—This is a "natural language" search engine that allows you to ask regular questions such as, "What's on television tonight in Minneapolis?" and get a list of appropriate Web sites. They are currently licensing the database engine underlying Ask Jeeves to other subject-specific sites.

DigiSearch (*http://www.digiway.com/digisearch*)— Searches up to eighteen search engines at once.

Dogpile (*http://www.dogpile.com*)—Simultaneously searches fourteen major search engines and many Usenet newsgroups.

Fusion (*http://lorca.compapp.dcu.ie/fusion*)— Searches six major search engines and fuses the results, increasing the quality of the search results.

IFind (*http://m5.inference.com/ifind*)—My search engine of choice. It always seems to give me the best results. I usually find what I'm looking for within the top ten listings.

Mamma (*http://www.mamma.com*)—Searches seven engines as quickly as you could search one.

Subject-Specific Search Engines

To discover industry-specific search engines and directories (discussed later), check out C|NET's search.com (*http://www.search.com*), which is actually a search engine for search engines. It will provide you with a list of specific search engines where you can submit your site. Also visit another such search engine, Internet Sleuth (*http://www.isleuth.com*). Finally, search in directories or indexes in the major search engines.

Here are a few subject-specific search engines:

Business Seek (*http://www.businessseek.com*)

Insurance Online (*http://www.insure.net*)

Money$earch (*http://www.moneysearch.com*)—Geared toward small businesses and online investors.

MRO Explorer (*http://www.mro-explorer.com*)— Features industrial manufacturers only.

Women Search Directory (*http://www.wwwomen. com*)—Focuses on women and women-oriented businesses.

Web Directories

People also use Web directories to find information on the Internet. The major directory, Yahoo, is as actively searched as any of the search engines. Following are some of the major directories (also known as indexes) where your site should be listed. Be sure to select your category very carefully. Check out the directory site before selecting the category for your site. It can make a difference in the number of people who discover your site.

Achoo (*http://www.achoo.com*)—Features health-related sites.

BizWeb (*http://www.bizweb.com*)—Click on the "Submit Your Company" link.

Business Classifieds (*http://www.bc-i.com*)—Click on "Add Listing."

ComFind (*http://www.comfind.com*)—Click on "Register Free Listing."

Eye on the Web (*http://www.eyeontheweb.com*)— This site provides "the tools to make your time on the Web as entertaining, interesting, productive, and meaningful as you want it to be." Submit your site by sending e-mail with your URL, a brief description of your site, and the category to: *submit@eyeontheweb.com*.

Galaxy (*http://galaxy.einet.net/galaxy.html*)

ISP Internet Yellow Pages (*http://www.index.org*)

Lexiconn (*http://www.lexiconn.com/dir*)—This is an index of businesses, organizations, and institutions. Click on the "Add URL" link to add your Web site.

The Link Engine (*http://www.1-web-bazaar-plaza.com/linkmat.html*)—This site features links in fifty categories, including cars, boats, pets, children, collectibles, games, and cooking.

LinkMonster (*http://www.linkmonster.com*)

Check out the directory site before selecting the category for your site. It can make a difference in the number of people who discover your site.

Rex (*http://rex.skyline.net*)—A service of the Internet Resource Exchange, Rex features thousands of Web sites. Click on "Add a Site."

Starting Point (*http://www.stpt.com*)—This site is one of the leading starting points on the Web.

The Virtual Tourist (*http://wings.buffalo.edu/world*)

W3 (*http://www.w3.org/hypertext/DataSources/by Subject/overview.html*)

Web411 (*http://www.sserv.com/Web411*)—This site is attempting to become one of the leading starting points on the Web. They screen sites before listing them. They do not list adult content sites or multi-level marketing sites.

Yahoo (*http://www.yahoo.com*)—The major directory on the Web, Yahoo gets as many hits as any search engine.

The Yellow Pages (*http://theyellowpages.com*)

Internet Malls

Internet malls are commercial Web sites that feature a number of specialized retail stores. Many of them accept free Web site listings. Here are a few of them:

Buy It Online (*http://www.buyitonline.com*)

Internet Mall (*http://www.internet-mall.com*)— Click on "Adding Your Shop."

ShopInternet (*http://www.ro.com/ShopInternet*)— This new site's goal is to list any Web site with something for sale.

WorldProfit Malls (*http://www.worldprofit.com*)— Click on "CashQuest" to feature your business

Internet malls are commercial Web sites that feature a number of specialized retail stores. Many of them accept free Web site listings.

for free in the CashQuest search engine. They currently list more than eight thousand sites.

"What's New" Pages

There are pages on the Web that only list sites that are new to the Net. EPage Classifieds (*http://ep.com*) let you take out a free classified ad announcing your Web site under the "Announcement" category. They can also create a free classified ad service for your site. Also check out their How to Announce Your New Web Site FAQ (frequently asked questions) at *http://ep.com/faq/Webannounce.html.*

Netscape, the most frequently visited site on the Web, has a What's New page at *http://www.netscape.com/home/whats-new.html.* The page features unique sites as well as sites that are good examples of well-executed Web design. Ketchum Kitchen's Web site had a tenfold increase in hits on the day it was featured on Netscape What's New (from four thousand average hits to more than *forty* thousand).

Open Market (*http://www.directory.net*) provides a daily listing of new commercial Web sites.

Web News Services

Many of the major search engines, as well as many other sites, offer news about the Web. Here are a few of those sites:

C|NET (*http://www.cnet.com*)—A division of the cable computer news show, this site features new sites and other Web news. It's also a good place to get the latest news and info on online marketing.

Internet Daily Report (*http://www.dbc.com/cgi-bin/htx.exe/newsroom/netdaily.html?source-core/dbc*)—This daily news service covers the Internet and has a readership of fifty thousand.

Net Profit Online (*http://www.net-profit.com*)—This subscription online forum discusses Internet business strategy. While a subscription costs $150 per year, the site does have some free services accessible to nonsubscribers.

Specialized Database Sites

There are many Web sites that list URLs for special-interest information. Here, for instance, are a few special sites where you might want to be listed:

ABA Bookstores (*http://www.bookweb.org/directory*) —If you have a bookstore, be sure to list your Web site at American Bookstore Association. You may have to join to be listed.

American List Counsel (*http://www.amlist.com*)— Features more than ten thousand mailing lists. If you offer mailing lists for rent, be sure you're listed here. If you are looking for lists to rent, look here also.

Catalog Mart (*http://www.catalog.savvy.com*)—If you have a catalog, be sure that you are listed here. Listings are free, but if you want the full treatment, you pay per response. BookPeddlers, a book publisher, pays $50 per month plus 25 cents per label to be linked back to its site. It averages about six hundred catalog requests per month.

CatalogLink (*http://cataloglink.com*)—Offers free listings of catalogs.

Edith Roman Associates (*http://www.edithroman. com*)—Offers a database of thirty thousand direct-mail lists. Be sure yours is listed if you have one. Other Web sites devoted to mailing lists include SRDS on the Web (*http://www. srds.com*) and Marketing Information Network (*http://www.dmnetwork.com*).

GuestFinder (*http://www.guestfinder.com*)—Another paid listing service for book authors and others who want to be featured guests and/or experts on a topic on radio and TV shows. Listings cost about $150 per year.

Newsletter Access (*http://www.newsletteraccess. com*)—Features five thousand subscription newsletters. If you publish one, be sure it's listed here.

ProfNet's Expert Database (*http://time.vyne.com/ profnet/ped/eg.acgi*)—You can search here for short biographies of two thousand leading experts from colleges and universities. Again, be sure to be listed if you qualify.

Seminar Clearinghouse International (*http://www. seminarnet.com*)—Allows seminar vendors to list their events for free.

Seminar Finder (*http://www.seminarfinder.com*)— Features thousands of seminars in the United States and Canada. Seminars are listed free.

Speakers Platform (*http://www.speaking.com*)—
Features many of the best speakers. Basic listings
are free.

Trade Show Central (*http://www.tscentral.com*)—
Features more than thirty thousand trade shows.

URL Submission Services

URL submission services allow you to submit to many of
the sites already mentioned (search engines, directories,
malls, and what's new pages) at the same time. While the
resulting listings from such broadcast services might not
be as complete as those you would submit individually to
each site, they do save you an incredible amount of time
and will get your site listed in some directories that you
might otherwise overlook. Here are a few of the free and
paid URL submission services (note that most of the free
services also offer more complete services or additional
services for a fee). You can find additional sites by searching Yahoo under "Announcement Services."

Add It (*http://www.liquidimaging.com*)—A free listing service.

Add Me (*http://www.addme.com*)—A free listing service that is quite good.

All-in-One Promotion (*http://www.erspros.com/
internet-promotion*)—This site offers sixteen hundred locations for submitting your site as well as
an Internet resources directory (for Web site design, development, and promotion) and a direc-

While the resulting listings from submission services might not be as complete as those you would submit individually to each site, they do save you an incredible amount of time and will get your site listed in some directories that you might otherwise overlook.

tory of sites looking for sponsors. Be sure to list your site here if you are looking for potential advertisers for your site.

Auto Submit (*http://autosubmit.com/promote.html*)—A free service.

Broadcaster (*http://www.broadcaster.co.uk*)—A free service.

Central Registry (*http://www.centralregistry.com*)—A free service.

Did-It.com (*http://www.did-it.com*)—This submission service also offers the Did-It Detective that allows you to find out how many sites took your listing and how many still need a nudge. You can use the detective service independently of the submission service.

Free Links (*http://www.mgroup.com*)—This free site allows you to post your Web site manually to two hundred sites.

Go Net Wide (*http://www.gonetwide.com/gopublic.html*)—A free service.

Incor's Free Classifieds (*http://www.incor.com*)—This free service submits your Web site to various classified ad sites.

Position Agent (*http://www.positionagent.com*)—This site offers a detective service similar to Did-It.com.

Qwik Launch (*http://www.quiklaunch.com*)—A free service.

Register It (*http://www.register-it.com*)—A free service.

Robo Submit (*http://www.inetwebs.com/ROBO*)—A free service.

Scrub the Web (*http://www.scrubtheweb.com/abs/ index.html*)—Click on "Easy Submit" for a free listing on the major search engines.

Submit-It (*http://www.submit-it.com/refer?1798*)— One of the first free listing services and still one of the best, it also offers expanded paid listings. Plus it has a referral program where you can earn money by referring others to its site.

WebSite Promote (*http://www.websitepromote.com*)— Sponsored by AAA Internet Promotions, this paid service will submit your site for you to many top search engines and directories. I paid to use this service to announce my Book Market Web site. They did a good job of getting the word out to two hundred other Web sites.

Web Step's Top 100 (*http://www.mmgco.com/top100. html*)—Sponsored by the Multimedia Marketing Group, this paid service offers the top twenty-five for free. It also offers a top two hundred service. It's another well-respected service.

Here are some more sites where you can submit your Web site for a free listing. A1 Index (*http://www.vir.com/ ~wyatt.index.html*) is a list of some 650 Web sites where you can announce your own site. It provides links, but you have to submit to each site separately. OnLine Business (*http://online-biz.com/links/freelinks.htm*) also features 650 sites where you can submit your site's Web address. Just for good measure, here are two more: PromoteOne (*http://www.promoteone.com*) and Web Site Promoters Resource Center (*http://www.wprc.com*).

Newsgroups

There are several Usenet newsgroups devoted to new Web sites. To submit to these newsgroups, you must use a newsgroup reader rather than a Web browser. Submit your site to the following announcement newsgroups:

> *news:bionet.software.www*
> *news:comp.infosystems.www.announce* (Before
>   submitting to this major announcement
>   newsgroup, read its charter on the Web at
>   *http://boutell.com/percent7Egrant.charter.*
>   *html.*)
> *news:comp.internet.net-happenings*
> *news:fj.netinfosystems.www*
> *news:misc.entrepreneurs*
> *news:tnn.internet.www*

E-mail Newsletters

Announce your existence to the e-mail newsletters that feature new Web sites. Keep in mind that with most e-mail newsletters, you must be a member of the list before you can post to it. Most offer a free subscription. Here are a few of the e-mail newsletters (sometimes also known as mailing list discussion groups or listservs):

> *Net-Happenings (http://www.mid.net:80/NET)—*
>   The archive of this newsletter is located on the
>   Web site listed here. To subscribe to this free
>   newsletter, send the following e-mail message

Announce your existence to the e-mail newsletters that feature new Web sites. Keep in mind that with most e-mail newsletters, you must be a member of the list before you can post to it.

to *majordomo@is.internic.net:* "subscribe net-
happenings" (without the quotes).

*Net Surfer Digest (http://www.netsurf.com/nsd/
index.html)*—You can subscribe to this e-mail
newsletter at the Web site.

Scout Report (http://scout.cs.wisc.edu/scout/report)—
Mails weekly to twenty thousand subscribers.
Submit site suggestions via e-mail to: *scout@
internic.net.*

Books That List Web Sites

Here are a few of the books that are continually updated
with new Web site listings. Be alert to news of other such
books, and try to get listed in the new editions of any
books on the Internet or World Wide Web.

*Free Stuff from the World Wide Web (http://www.
coriolis.com/coriolis)*—If you offer free reports,
directories, or other items on your Web site, let
them know.

*Internet Roadside Attractions (http://www.vmedia.
com/ira.html)*

*New Riders Official World Wide Web Yellow Pages
(http://www.mcp.com/nrp/wwwyp)*—E-mail
suggestions to: *internet@newrider.mhs.compu
serve.com.* This book features at least four
thousand Web sites.

*Walking the World Wide Web (http://www.vmedia.
com/shannon/shannon.html)*—Features extensive
descriptions of many Web sites.

Computer Magazines

Many computer magazines devote a section to Web site listings. In fact, there are now a number of magazines (such as *Internet User* and *Yahoo Internet Life*) that are devoted solely to the Internet. Be sure to let these computer magazines know about your new Web site. In fact, this opportunity to get notices in computer magazines is one of the main reasons you want to have a Web site, since these magazines could introduce your company or service to an entirely new audience. You can rent lists of computer magazines or develop your own list by searching various media directories at your local library.

You can rent lists of computer magazines or develop your own list by searching various media directories at your local library.

Special-Interest Magazines

For the past few years, while the Internet has still been major news, many special-interest magazines have featured news of Web site openings. Many special-interest magazines still feature such news. Your Web site opening will be another way to make the news in special-interest magazines for your product or service area.

General-Interest Magazines

The major news magazines as well as many other general-interest magazines still have sections that feature unusual online tidbits and news. *People* magazine, for instance, still has a "Bytes" section that features online tidbits.

Newspapers

USA Today and many local newspapers still feature new Web sites. Be sure to send news of your new site to all your local publications—daily, weekly, and monthly.

Send Releases via E-mail

Use one of the following e-mail news release services to let computer and online journalists know about your site. When you send out an e-mail news release, be sure to include your Web site URL and lead with a headline that features some benefit of your site.

Gina Internet Wire (*http://www.gina.com*)—Primary focus is sending tech-related news to thousands of technology media for approximately $179.

Internet News Bureau (*http://www.newsbureau. com*)—No personalization, but reaches thousands of editors for approximately $225.

PRNewsTarget (*http://www.newstarget.com/PRNews Target.htm*)—Best for technical products. A five-hundred-word release is sent to two hundred contacts for $395.

URLwire (*http://www.urlwire.com/uhome.html*)—Best resource for announcing Web developments and new Web sites. Sent to approximately three hundred contacts. Cost: $400 and up for personalized news releases.

Xpress Press (*http://www.xpresspress.com*)—Reaches eight hundred general media for about $150.

Other Online Directories

Get listed in other online directories. For instance, your college alumni association probably has an online e-mail and/or Web site directory. Check out my listing at my alma mater (*http://www.macalester.edu/~alumni*). Many other associations will have similar searchable listings. My publishing company, Open Horizons, is featured in the membership directory and links pages of the Publishers Marketing Association Web site (*http://www. pma-online.org*). Listings with the sites of professional associations and hobby organizations, of course, would be most useful for company owners, professionals, and service providers.

Post Messages to Newsgroups

There are thousands of newsgroups, each devoted to a different subject. You can read and post to these newsgroups without having to subscribe to them. Search for appropriate newsgroups using one of the search engines, and then join in the discussion. If you provide useful or entertaining information, people will begin contacting you for details. To ensure they can reach you, always include your e-mail signature with every post.

You can search for various newsgroups by subject using Yahoo (*http://www.yahoo.com/news/usenet*), Liszt (*http://www.liszt.com*), or Reference.Com (*http://www. reference.com*). Any of these services will allow you to find most of the newsgroups devoted to a specific topic.

Search for appropriate newsgroups using one of the search engines, and then join in the discussion. If you provide useful or entertaining information, people will begin contacting you for details.

As part of your research on newsgroups, check out DejaNews (*http://www.dejanews.com*), where you can search for past newsgroup postings by key word. For instance, enter your name into the Quick Search box, and you'll get a list of every post that has featured your name, including any post that included your e-mail signature. Do additional searches for your company name, brand names, generic product names, and any other key words related to your product or service. Then respond to the newsgroup messages that are returned by your search. Always send a response directly to the individual who posted the question or comment. And, if the response might be of interest to the entire newsgroup, send the message to the newsgroup as well. Keep a record of the search terms that drew the best response, because you will want to do such a search at least once a month. Note that the Excite and AltaVista search engines also allow you to search newsgroup postings by subject.

When Nan McCarthy self-published her first romance novel, *Chat* (written entirely in e-mail format), she had a hard time getting her book into bookstores. But she noticed that another book released at the same time was stacked high in pyramids at every store. The book? *Dave Barry in Cyberspace*. So she wrote a note to the humorist in the style of Dave's newspaper column. He replied with a short note telling her not to give up. Well, she didn't. She sent her humorous note to a number of humor newsgroups where Barry's fans congregate. And they responded. Soon she had sold out of the twenty-five-hundred copies she had printed and signed on with a

Driving Traffic to Your Web site

According to research conducted by Cahners Publishing, 49 percent of the readers of specialized business publications have visited a manufacturer's Web site in the last twelve months. How did they find out about Web sites? Most business Internet users learn about new sites through articles and ads in the trade magazines they read. Here are the sources Internet users cited most often:

74% trade articles

65% trade advertisements

59% links from trade magazine Web sites

58% word-of-mouth

35% trade magazine promotions

18% direct mail

computer book publisher to print another twenty thousand copies!

Post Messages to Mailing Lists

Unlike Usenet newsgroups, which are available for anyone to read and search past messages, mailing lists (also known as listservs) are available by subscription only. Most subscriptions are free, but you must be a member to post the group. Not only do I participate in the small press and PMA online discussion groups devoted to book publishing, but I also sponsor my own listserv devoted to book marketing (to subscribe, send the following e-mail message to *majordomo@bookzone.com:* "subscribe book-market"). I have become known on all three lists for posting useful information and providing practical answers to questions. As a result, I have sold many books and newsletter subscriptions and doubled my consulting business. To discover mailing lists that are devoted to a subject related to your business and Web site, search the following directories:

Liszt (*http://www.liszt.com*)—Features more than 71,600 mailing lists and 18,000 newsgroups.

Reference.Com (*http://www.reference.com*)—Besides mailing lists, this site also features newsgroups and Web forums.

Tile.net Lists (*http://www.tile.net/listserv*)—Only features those mailing lists operated by ListServ software.

Vivian's List of Lists (*http://www.catalog.com/vivian/interest-group-search.html*)—One of the original lists of lists.

Yahoo (*http://www.yahoo.com*)—Search for mailing lists or e-mail lists.

Submit Entries to E-mail Newsletters

Some mailing lists are actually moderated collections of content edited by an individual. These mailing lists welcome submissions and will allow you to post a little signature ad at the end of your message. For example, Ira Pasternack's *Marketing Tip of the Day* encourages submissions from its readers. More than a thousand Internet marketers currently read his newsletter, which we encourage

These e-mail newsletters welcome submissions and will allow you to post a little signature ad at the end of your message.

you to subscribe to if you are serious about marketing your Web site. To subscribe, send the following e-mail message to *majordomo@databack.com:* "subscribe mtotd" (without the quote marks).

Develop a Response Template

Design and save an e-mail message that you can use to reply to any unsolicited e-mail or to anyone requesting information. This response template should be headlined by a key benefit of your product or service, describe your product or service, offer one or two testimonials, make an offer they can't refuse, and make it easy for them to reply with a request for more specific information and/or to buy your product. Also include your e-mail and Web site addresses. Now, instead of trashing unsolicited e-mail or letting it pile up, send them your marketing message.

Design and save an e-mail message that you can use to reply to any unsolicited e-mail or to anyone requesting information.

Submit Your Site for an Award

Many sites and publications offer awards for the top Web sites, including Lycos's Top 5 percent of all Web sites, Magellan's 3-Star Site, *USA Today*'s Hot Site, Coca-Cola's 2000 Hotspot Award, IPPA Award for Design Excellence, and Microsoft Network's Pick of the Week. Once your Web site is established (and can be considered really hot or really cool), you might want to submit your site for an award. The easiest way to do this is to participate in AAA Internet Promotions Award Sites (*http://www.Websitepromote.com/traffic/award.html*). For $150, one of their professionals will nominate your site to the top fifty awards. Here, however, are a few sites where you can nominate yourself for an award (some of the other awards, such as Netscape's What's Cool section or Lycos's Top 5 percent, don't accept nominations):

Best of the Web (*http://www.botw.org*) — An annual
   award selected by visitors to the site. Winners are
   selected from five to ten nominees in each category.
Cool Site of the Day (*http://cool.infi.net*) — This oldest
   cool site selects a new site every day.
Jump City (*http://www.jumpcity.com*) — Reviews
   the best sites. Has featured sixteen hundred sites
   already.
Platinum 100 (*http://www.catalog.com/krs/plat.
   html*) — Top one hundred sites for the year selected
   by a panel of judges.
Web 100 (*http://www.web100.com*)

Submit Free Classified Ads

Search on any of the Web search engines for "free classifieds" to find places to submit these. Also, as mentioned before, Incor's Free Classifieds (*http://www.incor.com*) allows you to submit your Web site to various classified ad sites. Note that many classified ad sites delete ads that are more than a month old, so you might have to repeat this procedure on a monthly or bimonthly basis.

Caution: One new Web site posted classified ads at 107 different sites, which increased its site traffic by 15 to 25 hits per day but also resulted in 140 sales messages from those classified ad sites and only 7 requests for information (and no sales). Yet it had taken two people twenty-five hours to post those ads. Not a good deal.

Buy a Classified or Display Ad on the Web

For automobile dealers, there are a number of sites that will allow them to upload classified ads for used cars for a fee. For example, DealerNet charges $895 every six months for dealers to list their used cars on its service (which is also featured on Microsoft's CarPoint site). Since the average dealer spends $250,000 to $300,000 a year on marketing, this charge is small change to them. Similarly, Auto-by-Tel, the leading new car–buying service on the Web, charges their seventeen hundred dealers each several thousand dollars a year to have Auto-by-Tel refer online customers to them.

Advertise in Card Packs

These ubiquitous postcard mailings can be used to increase traffic to your Web site. Jeffrey Lant has been promoting his WorldProfit Malls via his Sales & Marketing Success card deck for several years now. As a result, the malls get more than 250,000 visitors every month.

Advertise on Billboards

Joe Boxer has displayed its Web site URL on a 6,000-square-foot billboard in New York City's Times Square.

Besides its Web address, the billboard also displays Joe Boxer's e-mail address and e-mail greetings from many of its customers (displayed on a 100-foot electronic zipper).

Advertise on TV

Besides using billboards, Coldwell Banker, a national real estate firm, broadcasts direct-response TV ads to promote its Web site and generate sales leads for its brokers. Its Web site, which features home-buying information and a database of listed properties, gets a major jump in traffic on Sundays when the spots air, as well as on Mondays when people access the site from their workplace computers. Coldwell Banker's Web site logs seventy to eighty thousand visitors every week and generates seven hundred to one thousand leads for its brokers.

Link TV to the Internet

Intel's Intercast technology allows users to receive TV broadcasts and Web pages simultaneously via cable, satellite dish, or antenna. When the home-shopping network QVC mentioned its iQVC Web site simulcasts during its TV broadcast, there was a fourfold increase in hits at the Web site.

Put Your URL on Premiums

PlanetOut, the largest gay-themed site on the Web, promotes its URL with imprinted pens, mousepads, buttons, and packages of condoms (which they give out at conferences).

Coldwell Banker's Web site logs seventy to eighty thousand visitors every week and generates seven hundred to one thousand leads for its brokers.

Advertise with U.S. WebLink Express

This service prints a Web directory that is included on a rotating basis in the Sunday supplements *Parade* and *USA Weekend*. The ads, which are seen in 770 weekend newspapers and reach 84.9 million U.S. households, feature paid URL listings at a cost of $4,000. For more information, check out their Web site at *http://www. weblinkexpress.com.*

Using Your Web Site to Market Your Web Site

Besides getting listed in all the right places and actively publicizing and advertising your Web site, you can also do things on your site to attract more visitors. The design of your Web site contributes a great deal to getting—and keeping—people there, but there are a few other things you can do on an ongoing basis to attract new and repeat visitors.

Establish Links with Others

Besides getting listed in the major search engines, having other sites link to you is probably the most effective action you can take to promote your site on the Web.

Besides getting listed in the major search engines, having other sites link to you is probably the most effective action you can take to promote your site on the Web. The best way to establish these links is to search for like-minded sites, ones that you would be proud to link to on your site. Then place a link to those sites on your site. Once you've done that, contact the other sites and ask them if they'd like to exchange links. Tell them that

Posting to Mailing Lists and Newsgroups

Here is an example of an informative post that quietly sells the copywriting skill of the writer Joe Vitale:

Dan Poynter and the entire parachuting industry has been jazzed all month because former president George Bush made a parachute jump—his second in his 73 years—this past week. It's had wall-to-wall news coverage. But few know the story behind the news. I want to bring it up here because I feel there are at least three lessons to be learned.

First lesson: Any event can be dramatized to get publicity. When Dan Poynter called me to help him promote the parachuting industry's conference here in Houston, I told him I was busy finishing up my new book but to call local publicist Linda Credeur instead. He did. But he never expected to get someone so attuned to media needs or media opportunities.

Linda heard Dan say—in casual conversation one day—that George Bush was the only president to ever parachute. A light bulb went on over Linda's head. She suggested they invite Bush to the convention, and even give him an award. Dan was reluctant, knowing Bush charged fifty grand to speak. I urged Linda to find a way to reach Bush, knowing he would attend for nothing if he were at all interested in parachuting. He was. And his appearance at the otherwise mediocre trade convention put that convention on the map. Four news crews covered the event. And the parachuting attendees couldn't believe their eyes or their luck when they saw Bush appear. Again, *any* event can be made media friendly with creativity and courage.

Second lesson: You never know what will happen as a result of your efforts. As a result of his appearance, Bush got excited about parachuting and said he wanted to make another jump (at age 73). Because his first jump was during World War II and not a pleasant memory for him, he wanted to bring closure to the past by doing the jump again, this time by choice. He did. And the media covered it all week. I saw a thirty-minute show on his jump Easter Sunday.

It was touching to see this man cry as he recalled the near tragic event from his past, and it was inspiring to see him *beam* as he jumped and floated to the earth. I told Linda Credeur that she changed history when she got him to attend the parachuting convention. Bush became the only president to ever jump *twice*, but more than that, she helped a man heal the past and feel "like a spring colt" (as Bush put it). That's an amazing and unforeseen event from just trying to get publicity.

Third lesson: Acknowledge the people who help you so they will help you again. I was not invited to the convention where Bush appeared (actually I was, but I didn't hear of the invitation until three days after the event). But what really got to me was that Linda Credeur, who planted the seeds for all of this to happen, was not involved or acknowledged when Bush made his historic second jump. She eagerly waited to hear when the jump would be. She had her media contacts sitting by their phones, waiting for her call to alert them. But when the jump was announced, Linda's name was dropped from the press releases and virtually no one involved her in the event. While publicists are often in the shadows and don't usually get media attention, not even having her name on the press releases that went out was in poor taste. I'm not suggesting Dan Poynter was involved in this, as I doubt that he was; Bush's jump was controlled by the government and the parachuting industry. But I do know that when key people are not acknowledged for their efforts, they are not keen to help again. The lesson here is to remember the people who help you move ahead.

I've written in detail about the Bush event because I knew quite a bit about how it came to be, and because I think there are lessons here for all of us.

Finally, if you want to talk to Linda Credeur about promoting your books for you, she's at 1-713-939-0680. I get nothing from posting her name and she doesn't know I wrote this.

Joe Vitale

jgvitale@ix.netcom.com - Direct response ads, sales letters & news releases

Latest book: CyberWriting: How to Promote Your Product or Service Online (without being flamed) (Bestseller at amazon.com) To order: 1-800-262-9699

NEW! - Visit The Copywriting Profit Center at http://www.mrfire.com

you've already linked to them but would appreciate a return link. When sending this message, provide them with the HTML text to link to your site. For example: <A HREF="http://www.bookmarket.com">Book Marketing Update</A>—Sell more books! Get a free subscription to the Marketing Tip of the Week.

Provide a Button Link to Your Site

When you offer to link with another site, you can also provide information on how they can download a graphic image representing your site. For example, software maker Syncronys refers potential link sites to a page on its Web site where it provides two buttons sites you can use to link to the Syncronys site (*http://www.syncronys.com*). Then they add the following note: "If you use our buttons on your site, thank you—and please let us know! Send a message to *RKurzer@Syncronys.com* with the URL, and we'll happily make your site a part of our Links Resources page! (Of course, sites with obscene, profane or otherwise dubious content will NOT be considered for inclusion in this program.)"

Find Out How Many Sites Link to Yours

Two of the search engines allow you to monitor how successful your linking program is by listing the sites that are linked to your site.

> AltaVista (*http://www.altavista.digital.com*)—Enter your Web site URL into the search form as follows: link:http://www.yoursite.com. The form will

return the names of the sites where links to your site were found.

Infoseek (*http://www.infoseek.com/Home?pg=ultra_ home.html*)—Click on "Link Search" and enter: link:yoursite.com.

Register with Missing Link

Missing Link (*http://www.igoldrush.com/missing*) collects and categorizes sites that will exchange reciprocal links with other sites. You can search the site for other sites to contact for exchanging links. You can also register on this site to seek others who want to exchange links. To register, you first have to add a link to Missing Link on your site.

Join a Web Ring

Web rings are collections of subject-related sites that are linked to each other in a ring—one site leading to another site, which leads to another, and so on. Besides going from one site to another, you can skip to random sites on the ring or get a list of sites on the ring. There are currently more than ten thousand Web rings featuring more than eighty thousand sites. You can hook up with a ring of sites, or you can sign up with one of the Web ring services:

Looplink (*http://www.looplink.com*)—This site allows you to sign up for one of about fifty Web rings that it maintains. Commercial sites are welcome. You also get one free monthly classified ad in Loop-link's e-mag (magazine distributed by e-mail).

There are currently more than ten thousand Web rings featuring more than eighty thousand sites.

RingWorld (*http://www.webring.org*)—At this site, you can sign up for one of many existing rings, although it discourages commercial sites.

Create a Web Ring

You can try to set up and manage your own Web ring in an informal way. Or, by the time you read this, the RingWorld site will allow you to create your own ring under its system.

Exchange Banner Ads

To increase your presence on another site, ask them to exchange banner ads (large horizontal rectangular graphics) with you. The banners, when clicked on, send people to your site via a hyperlink.

Join a Banner Exchange Program

There are a number of banner exchange programs you can participate in. These programs act as clearinghouses for Web sites that want to have their banners displayed on other sites. In return, each site in the exchange inserts HTML code to allow the banner exchange clearinghouse to rotate banners on its site. To find out more, visit these sites:

LinkExchange (*http://www.linkexchange.com*)—The Web's largest advertising network, it links more than 100,000 sites with more than four million banner views each day. Besides the free banner exchanges, you can also buy banner space via this network. In addition, you will be listed in the SurfPoint directory and be provided with the following statistics: number of times your site is visited, number of times your banner is displayed elsewhere, and number of times your banner is actually clicked on.

Links Banner Exchange (*http://www.villageonline. com/links/exchange*)—Another banner exchange network.

Sell Banner Ads on Your Site

Besides exchanging banner links for free, you can sell banner ads. The average ad rate is currently $40 per thousand impressions. If you want to sell ads on your site, be sure to evaluate the following points:

- What pages on your site have enough traffic or are targeted enough to be of interest to advertisers?
- Evaluate your site traffic. Check your server logs to discover how many people are coming to your site, where they are coming from, how much time they spend on your site, and which pages attract and/or hold their attention. Check out the services provided by Web Audit (*http://www.wish ing.com/webaudit/wa.html*) to help you to track

visitors to your site. Their suite of site auditing services costs $49.95 per year.

- Commission an independent site audit, which should reaffirm your analysis of your site and will also add credibility with potential advertisers.

- Determine how and/or who will sell ad space on your site.

- Develop a rate card, with cost per thousand, sponsorship opportunities, and other sales information.

- Evaluate how you will process and position the ads, what reports you can offer advertisers, how many times you'll show specific ads, and how you will track the response to ads. In short, you will have to develop or select software to help you carry out these important functions.

Hire a Web Advertising Network

If you want to make money by selling banner ads without going through a lot of effort, hire a Web advertising network. Also, check out these networks if you want to buy space on other sites. Online ads, according to research conducted by Find/SVP, shows that 39 percent of users clicked on an ad before making an online purchase. Here are a few networks to contact:

DoubleClick (*http://www.doubleclick.net*)—This network sells for some of the largest sites on the Web, from USA Today Online and AltaVista Search to Billboard Online and Travelocity. Unless your site

If you want to make money by selling banner ads without going through a lot of effort, hire a Web advertising network.

is getting thousands of hits a day, don't bother asking these people to represent you.

Infoseek Network (*http://info.infoseek.com/network*)—Besides selling banner ad space on your site, they also pay you cash for any referrals you make to their site (via their news feeds, directories, etc.).

Design an Effective Banner Ad

Most banner ads have a click-through rate of 1 to 2 percent. That means 1 to 2 percent of the people who see the ad go on to visit your site. What kind of banner ad is most effective? Here are a few tips on how to design an effective banner ad:

➥ Animated ads pull better than static ads, usually by 30 to 40 percent. In one instance, Icon CMT Corporation pulled response rates of 15 percent from its animated ad.

➥ Put the words "Click Here" somewhere in the banner. According to a recent study by Infoseek, a popular search engine, these words can increase click-through rates by 44 percent. Toshiba America found that this tip increased response rate to its ads to 5.7 percent on three search engine sites.

➥ Add color. Bold colors such as green and yellow outpull black-and-white ads.

➥ Larger banners pull a higher response (although banner ad size is becoming standardized).

➥ Banner ads should be changed frequently. Response rates drop by half once browsers have

Put the words "Click Here" somewhere in the banner. According to a recent study by Infoseek, a popular search engine, these words can increase click-through rates by 44 percent.

seen the banner several times. In Infoseek's experience, banner ads wear out after 200,000 to 400,000 impressions.

➠ Contests don't work. In an analysis of two thousand banners and half a billion impressions, Infoseek found no significant improvement in click-through for banners that featured contests.

➠ Simpler ads load faster and, thus, have more time to create an impression.

Pay for Key Word Banners on Hot Sites

Some of the major search engines (Excite, HotBot, and Infoseek) sell key words linked to your banner ad. If the key word you purchase is entered by someone using the search engine, your banner will come up. Such banner ads, while more expensive, are more likely to reach your target audience.

Develop a Chat Ad-bot

Black & Decker, for instance, has collaborated with Planet Direct to develop an advertising robot in the shape of a Dustbuster vacuum that pops up and volunteers cleaning tips and product information whenever someone in a Planet Direct chat group mentions dust or housekeeping. Thus far, these ad-bots only work in three-dimensional chat rooms, a rather new development for Web sites.

Join a Classified Ad Network

One such network is Classifieds2000 (*http://www.clas sifieds2000.com*), which currently features more than 150,000 listings and helps sell $3 million worth of goods each week. They have about thirty-five Web sites that offer direct access to the 150,000 classifieds via a search engine. They are looking for a few more strong partner sites.

Run a Contest

If you want to attract people to your site and keep them coming back for more, run an ongoing contest that requires them to come back to your site more than once. For example, Foghorn Press, publisher of outdoor recreation books, runs a favorite snapshot contest featuring people in the outdoors. The grand-prize winner, judged by the staff at Foghorn Press, will win a weekend getaway at Sorensen's Resort Cabins in the High Sierra. In another Web contest, Hotel Discounts' Trip from Hell contest drew tens of thousands of new visitors to its site. As a bonus, Hotel Discounts received hundreds of riotous tales of vacations gone bad—tales that were added to the site to give it additional content to attract more visitors.

If you want to attract people to your site and keep them coming back for more, run an ongoing contest that requires them to come back to your site more than once.

Donate a Prize for Another Site's Contest

When you register your site with Buy It Online (*http://www.buyitonline.com*), for example, you can also donate a prize for their Find Goober scavenger hunt (which requires people to visit three pages of your site searching for clues). As long as your prize isn't selected by a winner, your site link and prize graphic will stay at the site.

Set Up a Gift Registry

Just as stores attract gift buyers by setting up a gift registry, Web sites can do the same. For example, Ross-Simons, the jewelry and tableware retailer, offers a bridal registry on its Web site. The registry software is provided by Evergreen Internet, which also operates the All the Best gift registry. Harry & David, the specialty goods catalog, has set up a holiday gift registry, and Sur La Table, the kitchen products catalog, also plans to do the same.

Set Up a Guest Book

To capture the names, mailing addresses, and e-mail addresses of visitors to your site, encourage them to sign your guest book. Give them a reason: Offer them ongoing information whenever your site is updated, send them a monthly e-mail newsletter, or offer them a discount on orders. For example, Fisher Scientific offers a 20 percent discount certificate on Fisher purchases if people sign its site's guest book. Your Web site or Internet service provider should be able to help you set up a form that will allow people to easily sign your electronic guest book.

> **To capture the names, mailing addresses, and e-mail addresses of visitors to your site, encourage them to sign your guest book.**

License Useful or Entertaining Content

Cool Cards (*http://www.coolcards.com*) licenses its greeting card–creation software to other sites that, in turn, allow visitors to create their own e-mail greeting cards from the graphics available on the site.

Create Content for Other Sites

Another way to attract visitors to your site is to give some content (an article, graphic, or piece of software) to other sites. As mentioned earlier, the World Wide Information Outlet (*http://certificate.net/wwio*) and Article Resource Association (*http://www.aracopy.com*) both encourage additional contributions of articles to their sites, with full attribution to the contributor. My Book Market Web site features short articles that I requested permission to add to the site after seeing a post in a mailing list or newsgroup. I always give full attribution as well as a link to the site of the contributor. Check out the free reports on my site at *http://www.bookmarket.com/reports2.html*.

Create Your Own Content

For example, Mark Welch, a probate attorney in California, developed a directory of probate attorneys for the entire United States, listed by state (*http://www.ca-probate. com*). Guess who is at the top of the California list? Yes, it's Mark. Not only is his site bringing him many clients, but the traffic to his site is strong enough now for him to make additional revenue selling advertising.

Create Your Own Search Engine or Index

Make your search engine or index so good people will want to come to your site first to look for other links in your subject area. You can go two ways with an index: Offer a comprehensive index for your subject area or offer a select list (top twenty, top one hundred, and so on). BookZone, in its Literary Leaps index, is attempting to create a comprehensive index of all book-related sites. They currently have more than 1,500 sites listed. On the other hand, I took a more selective approach for bookmarket.com. I feature a select group of the top 101 sites in seven areas: publishing, book marketing, general marketing, Internet marketing, experts (focus on book authors and publishers), referral programs, and celebrations.

You can go two ways with an index: Offer a comprehensive index for your subject area or offer a select list.

Give an Award

Create a top one hundred list of sites devoted to your subject area or create some other sort of award. Then notify the sites that they've won the award and tell them how they can post the award logo to their site. You can send the HTML code with your message, so all they have to do is cut and paste the code onto their home page. Or you can tell them where to go on your site to grab the graphic and HTML code. Be sure to include a link to your site in the HTML code. When I created my top 101 indexes, I also designed award logos honoring those top sites. When I notified the award-winning sites, many of them linked back to bookmarket.com.

Sell Sponsorships

While 70 percent of online ad spending is on banners, 24 percent is spent on sponsorships of appropriate sites. Look for companies or sites that might be interested in sponsoring your site or parts of your site. Then contact them with a specific proposal. Give them a good reason to sponsor your site. For example, the new Ask Jeeves natural-language search engine is offering programs for companies that want to sponsor specific question categories.

Look for ways you can work with other site owners to add value to their sites while also adding value and traffic to yours.

Create Partnerships

Look for ways you can work with other site owners to add value to their sites while also adding value and traffic to yours. Recently Infoseek made a minority equity investment in Hoover's Inc., a publisher of reference materials for about ten thousand companies. As part of the deal, Infoseek has added an icon link on its home page to Hoover's site to give Web searchers faster access to financial statements, public offerings, stock quotes, and other data about the companies in Hoover's database. Hoover's information is also available through many other third-party sites, including America Online, Reuters, Dow Jones, Bloomberg, iVillage, and CNNfn.

Join Referral Programs

Use referral programs (also known as associates programs) to add content, value, and income streams to your site. Probably the best-known referral program is the one operated by Amazon.com, the Internet bookseller. Once you have officially signed up as an associate, Amazon.com pays a 15 percent commission for any book sales resulting from your referral. Amazon.com currently has more than eight thousand Web sites in its associates program, including Puppynet, Star Chefs, and *Atlantic Monthly*. Bookmarket.com features more information on the Amazon.com program as well as many other referral programs.

Set Up Your Own Referral Program

To drive traffic to your site, you might want to offer a referral program for other sites. To make a referral program work, your site has to sell something that other sites believe will attract visitors and generate response. Almost every major retailer on the Web now has or is working on referral programs. Below are a few of the other Web sites that currently offer referral programs. For a more extensive list, see *http://www.bookmarket.com/top101.html*.

> *Book Marketing Update* (*http://www.bookmarket.com*)—I offer referrers a free two-issue extension to their *Book Marketing Update* subscription for any referrals they make that result in a subscription order to the newsletter. This is a straightforward way to handle payments that gives referrers an immediate return on their referrals. In some of

To make a referral program work, your site has to sell something that other sites believe will attract visitors and generate response.

the other associate programs, you have to wait until you've accumulated many referrals before being paid anything.

CDNow (*http://www.cdnow.com*)—This music retailer offers two options: a cosmic credit program that offers referring sites credit toward buying items from CDNow and a merchandising partnership that pays larger sites a percentage of sales for referrals. CDNow has about two thousand sites signed up for its cosmic credit program and twenty-five sites for its merchandising program.

Submit-It (*http://www.submit-it.com/refer?1798*)—This Web site registration service pays referring sites whenever a referral orders one of Submit-It's paid programs. The information in the above URL (refer?1798) is my referral code. If you enter the URL as shown here and then go on to order one of Submit-It's services, I will be paid a percentage of the order. You can use a similar code to track referrals to your site if you decide to offer an associates program.

TravelBids (*http://www.travelbids.com*)—This online travel auction site offers a $5 referral fee for each registration resulting from a referral link. Since it costs someone $5 to register with TravelBids, the site is passing that registration fee on to the referring site in hopes that people will use TravelBids a lot in the future. Here's how their referral system works: For each site that shows TravelBids' logo, TravelBids sets up a unique registration page that includes the referring site's identification. Then, when a person registers with TravelBids, the ID is automatically entered into its database. They pay referring fees once a month.

Venture Communications Free Forum (*http://www.freeforum.com*)—They offer you 50 cents for every referral you send that results in an order for their free sample program.

Make a Free Offer

Advertise your free offer in news releases, e-mail updates, newsgroup postings, and Web links. Or pay FreeShop Online (*http://www.freeshop.com*) to feature your free offer. They charge you from $1 to $10 for every free request they process. They can also handle fulfillment of the offer.

Marketing via E-mail

Based on data collected by the U.S. Census Bureau, a recent study revealed that e-mail users make more money than nonusers. Executives who do not use e-mail earn an average of 10 percent less than those who use e-mail. Five years from now, every business card will carry an e-mail address. And most consumers in the United States will also have access to the Internet, either at home, at work, or both. It's no surprise, then, that many savvy companies are already looking to use e-mail as a way to market their products to their target audiences. In this section we will

Executives who do not use e-mail earn an average of 10 percent less than those who use e-mail. Five years from now, every business card will carry an e-mail address.

Indiscriminate mass e-mailings are known as spam and are not welcome (that means, don't spam!).

look at some of the ways businesses are already using e-mail to market their Web sites and their products.

Send Mass Mailings

Just as in direct mail, you can send out e-mail to thousands of addresses in a very short time. Indiscriminate mass e-mailings are known as spam and are not welcome (that means, don't spam!). But, if you develop a targeted list via the guest book on your Web site or via postings on news-groups and if you keep your message short, your mass e-mailing could produce returns as high as 9 percent. You can do such a mailing on your own, but most companies wisely choose to use an outside provider who will charge from 10 to 20 cents per address for mass e-mailings. Here are a few of the best-known mass e-mailers:

PostMaster Direct (*http://www.postmasterdirect.com*; 718-522-1531)—All their lists are 100 percent "opt-in." That means that people have chosen to be on their lists. They currently offer more than 4.4 million people on more than three thousand lists, with interests running from scuba diving to Java scripting. Using one of the PostMaster lists, Ichat rang up sales of $50,000 in five hours; in another mailing to thirty thousand members of the Web design and promotion list, Ichat saw its sales quadruple within four weeks. The BizWeb Gazette got a 14 percent response from another mass e-mailing. And Pride Vitamins got $3,000 in orders from a $600 mailing. Their message was

only three lines long. They sent prospects to their
Web site to close the order.

WebPromote (*http://www.Webpromote.com/de*; 888-
932-8600)—Also using only opt-in lists,
WebPromote offers more than four hundred categories to target.

Internet Media Group (*http://www.internetmedia.com*;
561-347-5060)—Collects names from a number
of sites and companies.

Electronic Direct Marketing (*http://www.edmarket
ing.com*; 888-551-7600)—Their toll-free 888
number is included in every mailing they send out
so recipients can call to take themselves off the list.

CyberPromotions (*http://www.cyberpromo.com*;
215-628-9780)—The president of this company,
Sanford Wallace, calls himself the king of spam.
Some sites are actively working to screen out all
mailings from this company. So be cautious in
using its list service.

Rent Out Your E-mailing List

Once you have developed a significant e-mailing list (five
thousand or more names), you can rent it out to others to
use. One of the best ways to do this is to work with one of
the companies listed in the above point. All of them can
build, manage, and broker your list. For example, under
PostMaster Direct's standard management agreement, they
provide you with forms and list infrastructure via their site.
They also provide marketing, mailing, merge/purge, and
subscribe/unsubscribe services. In return, they split list
rental income 50/50 with you. Note that with PostMaster

Once you have developed a significant e-mailing list (five thousand or more names), you can rent it out to others to use.

Direct, you can also earn free mailings by providing a link to their list sign-up form (for every sign-up not already on file, you can mail to eight people on PostMaster Direct's lists).

Research New Lists

Besides developing your own list via your Web site's guest book, you can also use some of the people-search services or yellow pages services to develop targeted e-mail lists. Here are a few e-mail directories that can help you develop a list:

InfoSpace (*http://www.infospace.com*)
Four11 (*http://www.four11.com*)
Bigfoot (*http://www.bigfoot.com*)

People expect a fast response to e-mail.

Answer Your E-mail

If you have a Web site and you place an e-mail address there for people to contact your company, be sure you answer that e-mail—and answer it fast. People expect a fast response to e-mail. Xerox Corporation, for instance, has generated global goodwill because Bill McLain, their "Voice of the Web," answers any question submitted to him, even if the question has nothing to do with Xerox or copiers. He answers about 350 questions per day. As for handling complaints, Bill says, "My style for complaint e-mail is simple. I assume that Xerox is at fault and try to help in any way I can." As part of his work, he has developed about eighty boilerplate responses, but he still responds personally to each question.

Always Provide an Option to Opt Out

When sending mass e-mailings, always offer recipients an option to get off your list and stay off it. In a test conducted by American List Counsel and Xoom Software, positive response increased by 51 percent when a company offered an opt-out option and an explanation as to why the e-mail offer was being sent.

Use an Autoresponder

To answer simple, routine questions, you might set up an autoresponder (an e-mail address that can automatically send a form message to anyone who sends e-mail to that address). For a sample of how it works, send an e-mail message to *bmusample@bookzone.com.* The autoresponder will send you back a sample copy of the *Book Marketing Update* newsletter. Your Web site host service should be able to set you up with as many autoresponders as you want. As an alternative, you can work with one of the following services:

DataBack Systems (*http://www.mailback.com* or
   e-mail: *services@mailback.com*)—This company
   provides autoresponder service at a low cost.

InfoPress Email-On-Demand (*http://www.castelle.
   com/email* or e-mail: *info@ibex.com*)—They also
   offer fax-on-demand services.

Other Uses for an Autoresponder

- ► Background news release information—When sending out news releases, especially to online media or media e-mail lists, you can provide them with additional background information via an autoresponder (as well as on your Web site).

- ► Catalog requests—Set up an autoresponder that people can use to request a printed or e-mail version of your catalog. Make this autoresponder available on your Web site as well.

- ► Sample issues—As mentioned earlier, I use an autoresponder to provide a sample issue of my *Book Marketing Update* newsletter.

- ► Updates—You could provide daily, weekly, or monthly updates about your products or other information to your customers, sales force, representatives, or other contacts.

Use E-mail to Broadcast a Fax

Several services allow you to send faxes to multiple addresses via e-mail. For more information on sending faxes over the Internet, check out *http://www.northcoast.com/savetz/fax-faq.html*, which provides information on commercial and free Web-to-fax services. Faxaway (*http://www.faxaway.com*) and Interpage (*http://www.interpage.net*) are two such services.

Offer E-mail Delivery of Web Page Changes

With new services such as Digital Bindery (*http://www.bindery.com*), you can offer Web site visitors daily or weekly delivery of specific Web pages with HTML code intact. PC World Online uses Digital Bindery to deliver daily updates of its Web site to subscribers. Other Web site publishers can offer their own free subscription service by registering with Digital Bindery.

Marketing via E-mail Newsletters

E-mail newsletters are one of the most important marketing tools available on the Internet. An e-mail newsletter is a periodic e-mail message sent out to a list of people who have chosen to subscribe. Most e-mail newsletters are

---

The Latest Advertising CPMs

According to research by Focalink Communications released in July 1997, the average Web ad rate was $39.53 per thousand impressions. But some Web sites can and do charge a whole lot more. Web serial sites, for example, charge an average CPM of $250.00. Such serial sites include soap operas, mysteries, and dramas on the Net. What's new sites that provide specific listings of new or recommended sites charge less than the average: only $30.27 CPM. Audio sites charge more: $63.93 CPM. If you plan to make money on the Net via advertising, you should consider which of these formats best suits your needs, skills, target audience, and income desire.

An e-mail newsletter is a periodic e-mail message sent out to a list of people who have chosen to subscribe.

free, but some do charge a subscription fee—a trend that may increase. However, since you would be using an e-mail newsletter to promote your product and Web site, you should probably offer your newsletter free.

Some newsletters, such as the *This Is True* newsletter, offer two versions, a limited one for free and a more detailed or more frequent one for a subscription fee. For $15, you can get a year's subscription to the full version of *This Is True*, which is sent out every week and does not include any third-party advertising. Or you can opt for the free version, which is sent out every other week, comes later than the paid version, does not include all of the listings in the paid version, and includes third-party ads. *This Is True* currently has 150,000 subscribers from 121 countries! And every issue, paid or free, includes promos for the two books that were compiled from previous issues.

How many Web sites do you know that get 150,000 hits every two weeks? An e-mail newsletter can be the best way to promote your Web site. Just listen to what Hal Croasmun, publisher of the *Build Your Business Daily Tips* e-mail newsletter, has to say about newsletter promotions:

We have had good response from search engines, banner ads, exchanging links, and posting to discussion lists. But the best response we have had comes from the community we are building with our online newsletter. It takes a lot of time and work, but by providing value to other people on the net, you can establish the kind of relationships that cause people to want to refer others to you.

To subscribe to his newsletter, send e-mail to *major domo@eden.com* with the following message: "subscribe byb" (without the quotes).

If you decide that you'd like to create your own e-mail newsletter, first consider what kind of newsletter or mailing list you want to create. Here are some options:

➤ A periodic newsletter—You can generate the content or solicit submissions from your readers or other experts.

➤ An alert service—You send out notices of Web site updates or other news from your company. Zondervan allows customers and media to subscribe to its E-Mail Alert Service, which provides information on its new and upcoming books.

➤ A public relations list—You send out a periodic e-mail press release to various media and/or customers. This is the kind of e-mail publication most Web sites offer when they have you sign their guest books. They send you periodic updates on new products, changes in products, or service updates.

➤ An unmoderated discussion list—Most mailing list discussion groups take this format. My BookMarket and BooksPR discussion groups are examples of unmoderated discussion lists.

➤ A moderated discussion list—In such a list, the list owner takes responsibility for editing all submissions to the discussion and sends out a daily or weekly digest. Adam Boettiger's Internet Advertising list is an example of a moderated discussion list. To subscribe to this excellent marketing discussion list, send the following e-mail message to *i-advertising@groupserver. revnet.com*: "subscribe" (without the quotes).

For most promotional purposes, you will want subscriptions to your online newsletter to be open rather than closed. "Open" means that anyone can join the list. "Closed" means that only qualified people can join the list. Open lists are far easier to administer since they can be done with list management software (such as Majordomo or ListServ).

To set up an e-mail list or discussion group, ask your site host service if it can manage your list. If not, check out Databack Systems. For more information about Databack's mailing list service, send e-mail to its autore-

Interstitial Ads

One of the latest developments in Web advertising is interstitial ads—commercial messages that appear during the download delay between one Web page and another. One company, Streamix Corp. of San Francisco, has developed new software that fills a Web browser's window with animation or videos during the delay between Web pages—without slowing down the download of the next page! Experts are already predicting that 20 percent of Web advertising dollars will go into interstitial ads during the next few years.

Berkeley Systems, using proprietary software, makes heavy use of interstitials in its online quiz show, You Don't Know Jack (http://www.bezerk.com). Interstitial ads pop up between every four questions in the fifteen-question quiz. Because of the intrusive nature of interstitials general advertisers are drawn to it. Advertisers on the You Don't Know Jack site have included 7-Up, Cuervo Tequilla, and Plymouth.

Larry Chase's Web Digest for Marketers

WELL, THAT WRAPS up another edition of WDFM. If you received this issue from a colleague and you wish to have your own free subscription, you can get that by visiting www.wdfm.com and filling in the very brief form.

Copyright notice: You can pass this issue of WDFM along provided you do not change the copy, you keep the opening and this closing material, and you notify Larry Chase at larry@wdfm.com. Larry Chase retains copyright of this material.

Cordially, Larry Chase, President, Chase Online Marketing Strategies

E-mail: larry@chaseonline.com | http://chaseonline.com

Voice: +01 (212) 876-1096 | Fax: +01 (212) 876-1098

Free subscriptions to Web Digest for Marketers: http://wdfm.com

Read my "10 Don'ts of Net Marketing" in NetGuide

http://techWeb.cmp.com/ng/dec96/fmrktng.htm

sponder: *md-info@mailback.com.* You will get a return message within minutes with all the information you need to set up an e-mail newsletter.

Here are a few of the ways you can use an e-mail newsletter to make money and promote your business or service.

Build Credibility with Customers

Larry Chase, president of Chase Online Marketing Strategies and publisher of the *Web Digest for Marketers* newsletter, gets 60 percent of his consulting and seminar business as a result of his monthly newsletter, which reaches seventy-five thousand readers online and in print (reproduced in *Advertising Age* magazine). He charges $500 for two hours of telephone consultation. Read the closing text for his monthly online newsletter on the previous page (note his subtle sales messages).

Offer a Two-Tier System

Offer two versions of your online newsletter; the first for free, the other for a price—just as *This Is True* does. Or use the online newsletter to provide samples of a paid printed newsletter. My *Book Marketing Tip of the Week* is used not only to promote my site, but also to provide samples of my printed *Book Marketing Update* newsletter.

Sell Ads

A travel sponsor to the Internet Sales mailing list received close to three thousand additional hits on its Web site, more than 250 e-mails, and $34,000 in sales.

Since most e-mail newsletters are focused on a special interest or audience, they offer advertisers highly targeted audiences. Rates vary from about $10 per thousand subscribers for general lists to about $20 per thousand for focused lists. Note that such ads can produce dramatic results. For instance, a travel sponsor to the Internet Sales mailing list received close to three thousand additional hits on its Web site, more than 250 e-mails, and $34,000 in sales. You can sell the ads yourself by contacting appropriate Web sites or other potential advertisers, or you can work with one or more of the following services:

ListExchange (*http://www.listex.com*)—This site features a list of e-mail newsletters that are looking to exchange advertising. Use this site to research potential advertisers or advertising opportunities. If you'd like to offer other sites ads in your e-mail newsletter in return for ads in their newsletters, you should register with this site. Registration is free. Use these list exchanges to help you build circulation for your newsletter.

AdNiche List—This e-mail newsletter from the Multimedia Marketing Group is sent only to e-mail mailing lists interested in accepting ads. AdNiche sends out news of companies wanting to buy ads, and members of the list can respond by sending their current advertising information and rates. To subscribe to this list, send the following e-mail message to *adniche@groupserver.revnet.com*: "join" (without the quotes).

Offer a Banner Ad Option

Besides offering advertisers sponsorship of your newsletter, you could also offer them a banner ad on your Web site, especially on the page or pages where back issues of the newsletter are archived.

Advertise in E-mail Lists

If you want to get more visitors to your site or more subscribers to your online newsletter, try advertising in related or noncompeting online newsletters. Again, you can use ListExchange and AdNiche to help you find the best places to advertise.

Contribute to Other Online Newsletters

Most online newsletters are always looking for good content. If you have some to offer, send it to the editor of the list. These online newsletters welcome submissions from outside individuals and will allow you to post a little signature ad at the end of your message that sells your service. For instance, the Internet Advertising list mentioned earlier encourages submissions from its readers and allows contributors to add a commercial e-mail signature to their message.

Do Market Research on the Net

There is an incredible amount of information out on the Web, but some of that data might be old or inaccurate (since much of the content is given away free).

You can do a vast amount of research via the Internet, from checking out potential media for advertising or publicity to researching potential markets for your products and services to developing lists of potential retail customers. Below are a few sites you might be interested in visiting. Start with these. Then check out the major search engines for others. There is an incredible amount of information out on the Web. Note, however, that some of that data might be old or inaccurate (since much of the content is given away free). When you find a site, try to determine how up-to-date its data is before relying upon that data, especially for critical mailings.

Media Research

Business News Media Directory (*http://www.
editpros.com*)—Features e-mail addresses
of business news editors at newspapers and
magazines.

Gebbie Online (*http://www.gebbieinc.com*)—This
publisher of media directories offers access to
many of its listings.

Magazine media kits (*http://www.magazine.data.com*)

MediaFinder (*http://www.mediafinder.com*)—A service of Oxbridge Communications, this service
offers access to more than eighty thousand magazines, newsletters, newspapers, directories, and
catalogs.

MIT Radio Stations List (*http://wmbr.mit.edu/stations/
list.html*)

News Resource (*http://newo.com/news*)—Lists newspapers with Web sites.

Parrot Media (*http://www.parrotmedia.com*)—
Features addresses of radio and TV stations as
well as special-interest editors at newspapers.

Publicity on the Internet (*http://www.olympus.net/
okeefe/pubnet*)—Offers hundreds of links for
Internet promotion opportunities.

Radio Directory (*http://www.radio-directory.com*)

U.S. All Media E-Mail Directory (*http://www.edit
pros.com*)—This site offers access to the most
extensive list of e-mail addresses for media.
Listings also include mailing address and phone
numbers.

Market Research

You can use any of the yellow pages directories (such as Big Yellow at *http://www.bigyellow.html* and Big Books at *http://www.bigbooks.com*) to research business listings in almost any category, from floral shops to music stores. Most major search engines offer ready access to at least one of the yellow pages directories. Here are some more:

Catalog Mart (*http://www.catalog.savvy.com*)—A great site for looking up catalogs to sell your product.

CatalogLink (*http://cataloglink.com*)—Another good site for researching catalogs.

Federal statistics (*http://www.fedstats.gov*)—This U.S. government Web site allows you to search statistics from seventy agencies, including the Census Bureau.

PetSmart (*http://www.petsmart.com*)—A chain of pet stores.

Trade Show Central (*http://www.tscentral.com*)— Features more than thirty thousand trade shows.

Supplier Research

Thomas Register of Manufacturers (*http://www.thomas register.com*) offers a free database of 155,000 manufacturers. For a complete and updated list of more sites like this, check out my Marketing Top 101 list at *http://www.bookmarket.com/top101*. You can use many of these sites to assist you in carrying out the tips in the next section of this book.

5

Forty-Eight Low-Cost, High-Impact Promotional Ideas

Acting on a good idea is better than just having a good idea.

—Robert Half

N ow that we've covered direct marketing via the 9/18 Relationship Marketing System, publicity, and Internet marketing, we'd like to finish up by presenting a collection of other great low-cost, high-impact marketing ideas. These ideas should stimulate your thinking and help you generate plenty of ways to market your product, service, organization, or idea. Select the two or three ideas presented here that you think would work best with what you are offering as well as the skills, time, and money you have to put into promotion.

Idea 1: Become a Speaker

One of the best ways to promote any product or service is by speaking. Not only does it cost very little, if anything, but in some cases you will actually be paid to speak—and, at the same time, have a chance to promote your product or service. To build some experience and refine your basic speech, start by contacting your local Rotary, Lions, or Kiwanis club, all of which are hungry for new and interesting speakers. Talk to the person responsible for getting speakers and provide him or her with a list of talks you can give. You might start with a list of two to five talks (they can cover the same subject, but under different headlines). Come up with good titles for your talks—titles that will attract attention and cover an area that ties in closely with your product or service specialty.

When giving your speech, integrate mentions of your product or service. The best way to do this is to tell anecdotes from your business experience to illustrate your major points. When I talk about book marketing, I often draw upon my experience in publishing and promoting *1001 Ways to Market Your Books*, especially when talking about creating a good product and generating word-of-mouth.

Before your talk, ask the person who will introduce you to announce that you will be available afterward to speak to anyone with any additional questions. Be prepared with plenty of business cards, fliers, and brochures to give out to the people in attendance. Whenever possible, pass out these materials before the talk; you will

> To build some experience and refine your basic speech, start by contacting your local Rotary, Lions, or Kiwanis club, all of which are hungry for new and interesting speakers.

probably be inundated with people wanting to speak with you afterward. If you include some points from your speech or a list of resources that the audience can follow up on later, they are more likely to take your brochure home with them.

Better yet, give something free to everyone who attends your lectures. Art Fettig of Growth Unlimited offers everyone a free copy of one of his verses, illustrated and ready for framing. Each verse has his name, address, and phone number. He gets many bookings and book sales through this means alone.

Other places you might want to give a lecture: bookstores, clubs, churches, civic groups, Chambers of Commerce, schools, colleges, PTAs, writers' clubs, garden parties, business group luncheons, workshops, seminars, professional meetings, cruise ships, museum shows, conferences, ski lodges, and anywhere else that welcomes speakers and entertainers. The Indiana Chamber of Commerce has set up its own speakers bureau. Check to see if your own local or state chamber has a similar program. Also, the program chairs of your local Toastmasters Speakers Bureau meet monthly to exchange names of good speakers and to hear presentations from new speakers. Why not track down your local Toastmasters group to see if you can speak to them?

If the subject of your talk is of interest to a specific national association with local chapters, why not set up a speaking tour with these local chapters? Linda Salzer, author of *Infertility: How Couples Can Cope*, funded her lecture tour by visiting local chapters of Resolve, the national support group for infertile couples.

> The program chairs of your local Toastmasters Speakers Bureau meet monthly to exchange names of good speakers and to hear presentations from new speakers.

As you travel, plan ahead. Try to arrange speaking engagements wherever you travel. Beverly Nye, self-publisher of *A Family Raised on Sunshine*, bought a thirty-day bus pass to tour five cities where she had previously lived. In each city she arranged with Mormon church groups and homemaking classes to give lectures, where she talked about her own methods of homemaking. Not only did she make money on the admission fees charged for the lectures, but she also sold more than 1,500 copies in thirty days.

Remember, as a professional you should also charge to speak at major seminars, conferences, club meetings, and so on. These fees will help pay your way for other speaking engagements and help to keep your promotional show on the road.

Finally, if you are speaking at a newsworthy event, let the media know. Also, send them an advance copy of your lecture so they can quote from it accurately if they decide to cover the event.

> A good number of self-promoters have found that lecturing at colleges and adult education classes is an excellent way to market their products and services.

Idea 2: Become a Teacher

A good number of self-promoters have found that lecturing at colleges and adult education classes is an excellent way to market their products and services. Opportunities for such classes are all around you: at local colleges and universities, secondary schools, technical schools, Learning Annex, Open University, Unity Churches, and many other places.

Melvin Powers, publisher of Wilshire Books and author of *How to Get Rich in Mail Order*, has taught for many years in the California college system. Not only does a description of his course get mailed to a million-plus potential students, but in the course description he recommends that students read his own book ahead of time. He suggests that students buy the book at a local bookstore or check it out of their library. As he notes, "The result was phenomenal from a standpoint of sales."

Local chefs in many cities promote their restaurants by teaching at the Learning Annex or other adult education sites in their area. When people have a chance to taste your cooking while you are teaching them, they are far more likely to visit your restaurant. In the same way, job search consultants, psychologists, business consultants, and others can promote their services while giving people a taste of their knowledge.

As in promoting speaking opportunities, be sure to come up with a good title for your class. Offer something free for them to take back with them. And encourage participants to come up and talk with you after class.

Idea 3: Write a Column

Columns are a great way to get regular exposure to a targeted group.

To gain greater visibility, write a regular column for an appropriate trade journal, newsletter, or local newspaper. Columns are a great way to get regular exposure to a targeted group. If you're not comfortable writing a column by yourself, work with a freelance writer to put the shine on your ideas.

For instance, Luther Brock, a direct-mail copywriter, writes regular columns for *Direct Marketing*, *Mail Order Connection*, and other publications. He does no advertising—his columns bring him all the business he can handle.

As we've traveled around the country, we've noticed many newspapers featuring weekly columns by local gardening experts, real estate agents, restaurateurs, decorators, relationship counselors, and travel agents. If your local metropolitan daily newspaper isn't open to publishing a regular column by you, try the weekly alternative newspaper (such as the *Chicago Reader*, *River City Times*, or *Phoenix New-Times*) or monthly giveaways (such as the many parenting or computing newspapers now popping up in free newsstands around the country).

Idea 4: Write Articles

If you are not up to writing a regular column every week or month, try to work up an article once or twice a year. Any such promotion will help get you more visibility.

Idea 5: Do a Radio Show

If you are more comfortable chatting with people than writing articles, talk to your local talk-radio station about doing a weekend show on your specialty. Many talk stations offer locally generated shows on weekends. In Des Moines, for instance, WHO radio has shows on gardening, relationships, careers, home repair, and investments—all hosted by local experts. Become the house doctor or gar-

Become the house doctor or gardening wizard for your area, and watch your sales grow!

Magazines Want Your Expertise!

Most business magazines are hungry for articles written by people in the business. Below, for instance, are just a few of the articles featured in the July 1997 issue of Incentive magazine. In each case, the magazine also listed information about the author, his or her company, and contact information.

➡ A feature article, "Looking for a Workplace Role Model?" written by William Kalmar, director of the Michigan Quality Council.

➡ A sidebar, "More Time, Less Stress," reprinted from Patricia Haddock's booklet, 84 WorkSmarter Tips Guaranteed to Put More Time in Your Life.

➡ A Leadership Lessons column by Stephen Covey, head of the Covey Leadership Center and author of The Seven Habits of Highly Effective People. Covey writes a one-page article each month for Incentive.

➡ A sidebar on "Creating the Ultimate Sales Team" featuring a short interview with Kevin Carroll, owner of Corporate Capers.

➡ A short article on "Positive Performance Reviews" by Ernest Oriente, founder of PowerHour, a professional business coaching service.

➡ An article that incorporated thirteen guidelines for designing coupons based on a submission from CMS Inc., a coupon design company.

➡ A short note about boosting Web site traffic featuring a survey conducted by the Institute of Management and Administration.

dening wizard for your area, and watch your sales grow!

Many stations are looking for new shows. Look for a station with a gap and then approach its program director with your show idea. If he or she balks, offer to help the station sell ads for the show. Or, if your budget allows, buy the airtime and sell the ads yourself (so you don't lose money). You'd be surprised how inexpensive weekend airtime can be.

Idea 6: Become a Joiner

Do anything you can to become visible. This means joining appropriate trade and social associations related to your topic (if you don't already belong). But don't just sign up; become active in the association's activities. If you were interested enough in a particular field to form a company, you should be interested enough to become active in working with a related association. Such associations are incredible places to begin networking. You'll meet all sorts of prime contacts at association events.

That's why I am a member of the Mid-America Publishers Association. And it is also why I was a member of its board of directors for four years—not just because it's good for business, but because the problems and possibilities of smaller book publishers concern me. As a member, I have been invited to speak at the association's annual meetings many times. And, whenever I send in a news item related to my books and services, the MAPA newsletter prints it. Neither of those things would happen if I were not active in the association.

Idea 7: Become an Expert

As a service provider or producer of a product, you automatically become an expert in the subject related to your

Don't answer a reporter's questions if you don't know the answers. Admit the limits of your expertise if you want to become quoted as a reliable source.

company. However, to become recognized as an expert, you must also establish yourself as a reliable source of news or information. That means sending out regular press releases and news stories. It also means not claiming more knowledge than you have. Don't answer a reporter's questions if you don't know the answers. Admit the limits of your expertise if you want to become quoted as a reliable source. And whenever possible, refer reporters to someone who can answer their questions. To help you make those referrals, develop a database of people, companies, and organizations in your area that you feel comfortable recommending. Then ask them to do the same for you.

As an author of a number of books about publishing, I am often called upon to consult with smaller publishers and nonprofit associations about book production and marketing. I help where I can, and when I don't know the answer I send them to people who can help them. In the same way, many editors and publishers have sent people my way because they knew I could answer the questions from their readers. The best part? I've received many book orders and consulting jobs from these referrals.

Idea 8: Become a Talker

Talk to anyone and everyone you meet. As a self-promoter, you should not hesitate to talk about your work. Let people know what you do. In many cases, they might have need of your service or product. To have this work, you must go out of your way to talk to people. And you must enjoy talking to them.

Strut Your Stuff!

If you want to achieve success in any field, you have to become a talker, you have to be willing to put yourself on the line. When movie director Garry Marshall was out on the road promoting his autobiography, <u>Wake Me When It's Funny</u>, a good number of people tried out for parts in his new movie, <u>Dear God</u>, while seeking his autograph. Thirteen of these acting hopefuls actually got parts in the movie. What would have been their chances if they had waited for a casting call? Almost nil.

One author of a guidebook for handicapped travelers happened to sit next to Abigail Van Buren on an airplane flight. Of course, during their conversation the author mentioned her book. Some time later, Abigail found an opportunity to write about the book in her syndicated column, "Dear Abby." The result? Two huge sacks full of mail for the book publisher—all orders.

An author of a book on relationships sold a copy of her book to everyone in the first-class section of a flight from Chicago to New York. One of the pilots and two flight attendants also bought copies. If the flight had been longer, she would have sold even more copies, but she didn't have time to hit the passengers flying coach.

Idea 9: Leave Parts of Yourself Behind

As you move around in your day-to-day activity, carry extra copies of any promotional brochures, fliers, and news releases about your product or service. Give these away to people you meet. Leave some lying around the doctor's office, in the laundromat, on the bulletin board at your local grocery store, in a local restaurant, at the airport, and wherever else you go—especially places where other people have to wait and are, therefore, likely to be looking for some reading material to pass the time.

Here are a few other parts of yourself that you can leave behind:

➡ If your products are stocked by your local retailers (and they should be!), print up some stickers or cards that point out that you are a local manufacturer. Ask the stores if they would mind if you placed these stickers on the copies of your products in stock. Almost all of the stores will appreciate this extra effort.

➡ Offer to autograph the stickers as well. As signed editions, the products are more valuable—and, thus, more likely to be bought.

➡ Give fliers or brochures to the people at the cash register—or the person in the store most likely to have contact with potential buyers.

➡ Above all, leave a good impression. Wherever you go, dress well, speak well, and act with good manners.

Idea 10: Personalize Your Promotions

When you send promotional material to retailers and distributors, send them a personal note as well. Such personal touches help to get your material to the top of the stack—and read! Indeed, Dan Berger, book buyer for the Raleigh News Company, has said as much. He definitely pays more attention to personalized promotional material, especially if it's newsy and interesting.

You might want to publish a promotional newsletter (two or four pages), which you could send to retailers, wholesalers, clients, media, and opinion leaders. Keep them up to date on any new promotions, publicity, and sales that might encourage them to take a second look at your product or service. Again, put some of yourself into the newsletter. Let them get to know you as well as your product or service. You might want to feature one of your employees in every issue. Use their story to highlight one of your strong selling points (for instance, by telling how one employee went out of his way to make sure a customer was satisfied with her order). Such stories not only sell your company to your customers, but also reward your employees when they do a good job.

> **Put some of yourself into the newsletter. Let them get to know you as well as your product or service.**

Idea 11: Sell Door-to-Door

Don't laugh. Door-to-door selling can be an effective way to sell your products or services. It's not the easiest way to sell but it's a wonderful way to introduce yourself to a community. For instance, if you open up a new pizza place, walk around the neighborhood to personally deliver your opening-day coupons (or, better yet, samples of your pizza). Communicate your excitement and invite

If you are a bug exterminator, lawn mower, résumé writer, home decorator, or other local service, take time to introduce yourself to people.

them to your restaurant as your guest. You'd be surprised how many people will take you up on your offer. One Chinese restaurant owner dressed up in a suit and visited all the real estate agents within two miles of his new restaurant. By offering a sample of his food and a menu, he soon built up a large lunch and dinner trade.

Service providers can do the same. If you are a bug exterminator, lawn mower, résumé writer, home decorator, or other local service, take time to introduce yourself to people. Don't just leave fliers hanging on doorknobs. Ring the doorbell and talk to people. Even if they have no need for your services, someone they know will have such a need. And, again, if they know you, they are far more likely to recommend your service over someone else's. A chiropractor who wanted to open a new office in an area where many chiropractors were already well-established first spent three months knocking on twelve thousand doors. During that time, he was able to invite more than sixty-three hundred people to his open house. As a result of his door-to-door efforts, he saw 233 patients and earned more than $71,000 in business income in his first month. All it took was his time (ten hours a day for three months), but he established a flourishing practice.

Of course, you can also go for the direct sale of your product or service. Gary Provost, author and publisher of *The Dorchester Gas Tank*, began his career selling direct to his readers. He'd take a suitcase of books to downtown Boston every day, settle down at some busy corner (around City Hall, the public library, a subway entrance, or plaza), and begin peddling his books to anyone who'd listen. He'd sell twenty to twenty-five books a day. That's more sales than most authors make per day. Why couldn't you do the same with pizza, manicures, widgets, or other products and services? There's nothing stopping you once you resolve to enthusiastically promote and sell your product this way. But please do check local laws before selling or promoting anything door-to-door.

Idea 12: Form Alliances with Others

Besides joining organizations, you should also try to work out arrangements with related local companies as well as with services in other parts of the country to promote each other's work in your home areas. See the boxes on the following pages for information on forming alliances.

Idea 13: Set a Record

One way to get publicity for your product or service is to set a world record (a record that can somehow be related to your company). Note that you don't have to set a world record to gain publicity, you only have to attempt it. Actually, if you're not into setting world records, you could sponsor an attempt or announce a contest and prize for such an attempt—anything at all that associates you and your company with the world record.

For more details on how to get into the record books, read Clint Kelly's book, *The Fame Game*, available from Performance Press, P.O. Box 7307, Everett, WA 98201.

Cross Promotions That Work

➤ When MCI teamed up with major airlines to offer frequent-flier miles for placing long-distance calls, their business grew quickly.

➤ When Primo's coffee shops of San Francisco developed a partnership with Sweet Charlotte candy shops to sell each other's products, the two companies ended up developing a plan to test-market a chain of cafés that featured both candy and coffee.

➤ When seven home-owned toy shops in Massachusetts were faced with increased competition from several big toy chains, they formed a marketing partnership where they hosted promotional parties, joint raffles, bulk discounts, and a collective frequent-buyer card. In addition, whenever one of the stores didn't have a toy in stock, they referred their customers to one of the other stores in the partnership.

What does it take to create successful cross promotions? Here are a few of the characteristics you should look for in a promotional partner:

❑ Is the partner a natural fit with your business? Don't try to stretch too far from your special area.

❑ Do you want to link your reputation with your partner's reputation? Be sure to choose a company you trust.

❑ Look for companies that can offer you something extra: a wider audience, new marketing channels, enhanced credibility.

❑ Look for companies that are about the same size as your company. Don't get involved in a lopsided partnership. Make sure the contributions to the partnership are about equal.

How to Form Alliances

- When visiting retailers and distributors, always make sure they stock not only your product but also the products of the others with whom you are working. You might even act as each other's sales agents in a particular area of town or region of the country.

- Leave promotional material for each other wherever you go. Or, if you have a retail store, you can trade coupons with a related store. For instance, a garden supply store might give out coupons for a lawn-mowing service while the mowing service gives out coupons for the store. One health club saved a fortune in advertising costs by working with health food and sports shoe stores to give away free six-week health club memberships with any purchase. The stores gained from an added sales benefit and the health club got free advertising.

- Co-publish a newsletter that carries news and features about each company or service.

- Publish a mail-order catalog that features products from any number of related companies and then have each company mail the catalogs to their customer list. Orders could go directly to each company or be handled by one company on behalf of all the companies.

Idea 14: Do It for Charity

While you are attempting the world record or while you are doing other promotions for your company, do them for a charitable cause. Not only will this help you get publicity, but at the same time you will be doing a good turn for the charitable cause by drumming up publicity (and money) for it as well.

Kathryn Leigh Scott has sold her book *My Scrapbook Memories of Dark Shadows*, to several public television stations to use as a premium in their annual pledge drives. As part of the deal, she spent several days shooting generic spots for pledge drives across the country.

Foghorn Press of San Francisco publishes all its outdoor recreation books in cooperation with a nonprofit organization like the Sierra Club or Save the Whales. For every book sold, the publisher donates a small percentage to the nonprofit group. In return, Foghorn gets the added promotional uplift from the nonprofit associations (and media are more likely to feature the press's books since a portion of the profits are going to a good cause), often makes additional sales to the association, and gets to print the organization's logo on the cover of the book.

Idea 15: Sell to Associations

Even if you don't work directly with a charitable organization, there are many ways to work with associations to sell or promote your products and services.

Even if you don't work directly with a charitable organization, there are many ways to work with associations to sell or promote your products and services. Send news releases to their newsletters. Rent their membership lists for your direct-mail programs. Join them in a joint promotion. Advertise in their newsletters and/or membership directories. Be sure that your directory listing mentions your product or service. Attend their annual conferences or other events. Display at those events. Speak at those events. The opportunities for networking and promotion in the nonprofit world are endless.

For a list of national associations, check out the *Encyclopedia of Associations* (Gale Research) or the *National Avocational Organizations* and *National Trade and Professional Associations* directories published by Columbia House. Most libraries carry at least one of these directories. For local associations, check your yellow pages or Chamber of Commerce.

Idea 16: Sell or Donate to Fund-Raisers

Schools, churches, bands, scouting groups, and clubs often sell products as a means of raising money. Groups sell books, magazines, candy, cookies, T-shirts, coupon books, and other products to raise money. Why not offer your product to be sold in such a fund-raiser if it fits the organization's purpose?

If you have a service, you might want to develop a coupon or packet of coupons that they can sell rather than give away. For instance, if you are a dry-cleaning service, sell the organization a packet of discount cleaning coupons worth $25 or more. Sell the packet to the group for $2 or $3 and encourage its members to resell the packets for $5 or $10. It would be a great way to get your coupons distributed and, once people had paid for the packets, they would use them (not always the case with free coupons).

If your products or services aren't appropriate for fund-raisers, you can often donate them for fund-raising auctions, pledge campaigns, or other such events. Check with your local public broadcast station, PTA, garden

If your products or services aren't appropriate for fund-raisers, you can often donate them for fund-raising auctions, pledge campaigns, or other such events.

club, band, or other group for its next fund-raising event. While you won't make any money on such donations, you will get public recognition as well as the word-of-mouth publicity that results from someone selling or raffling off your product.

Idea 17: Sell to the Government

Every local, state, and federal governmental unit needs to buy products and services from private companies. The federal government alone is a $200+ billion market. If your product or service fills a need, check out the requirements for bidding on government work. For local governments, you can go down to City Hall or the county courthouse and ask around. You'll eventually find someone who can tell you how things work. You might also check with the Chamber of Commerce.

For federal sales, here are a few resources that can help you:

Government Product—News Penton Publishing, 1100 Superior Ave., Cleveland, OH 44114; 216-696-7000; fax: 216-696-7658. This monthly magazine is sent to government executives, administrators, engineers, and purchasing officials.

Doing Business with the Federal Government—This forty-eight-page booklet tells how to bid on government procurements, market products to federal agencies, and deal with government procurement agencies. It is available for $2.50 from

While you won't make any money on donations to fund-raisers, you will get public recognition as well as the word-of-mouth publicity that results from someone selling or raffling off your product.

the Consumer Information Center, P.O. Box 100, Pueblo, CO 81002.

Getting Started in Federal Contracting—This is a useful book for those who want to offer manufacturing, construction, or consulting work. Available from Panoptic Enterprises, P.O. Box 1099, Woodbridge, VA 22193; 703-670-2812.

Idea 18: Sell to Mail-Order Catalogs

While the major mail-order catalogs drive a hard bargain—requiring an effective discount that can run as much as 60 to 70 percent—they can move a lot of product. Not only that, but the exposure they give your product to their large customer base will often result in spillover sales through retailers. Where else could you find outlets that are willing to pay you so they can advertise your books to as many as five million people?

There are some six thousand companies in the United States that sell products through catalogs. In 1987, they mailed more than fourteen billion catalogs. In that same year, catalog sales topped $40 billion ($30 billion for consumer goods and $10 billion for business goods).

Catalogs can be broken down into a number of different categories. Here are a few of the major categories:

- **General** Lillian Vernon, Miles Kimball, Walter Drake, Harriet Carter.
- **High-ticket** Bloomingdale's, Neiman-Marcus.

While the major mail-order catalogs drive a hard bargain—requiring an effective discount that can run as much as 60 to 70 percent—they can move a lot of product.

➡ **High-tech** Edmund's Scientific, Sharper Image, Power Up, ComputAbility, MicroWarehouse.

➡ **Games and novelties** Brainstorms, Johnson-Smith, Whole Mirth, Loompanics.

➡ **Children's** Toys to Grow On, A Child's Collection, FAO Schwarz, Just for Kids, KidsRight, My Child's Destiny, Constructive Playthings.

➡ **Cooking** Jessica's Biscuits, Kitchen Arts and Letters, Wine and Food Library.

➡ **Business** Quill, Reliable, Viking, Whole Work Catalog.

➡ **Catalogs for professionals** Robert Anderson Publishing (health care), Mix Bookshelf (music/broadcast), Firefighter's Bookstore (firefighting), Jax Photo Books (photography).

➡ **Specialty items** Brookstone and Tools for Living (tools); Lee Ward, Dick Blick, and Boycan's (crafts); Dance Mart (dance); Genealogist's Bookshelf (genealogy); GolfSmart (golf), J. C. Whitney (auto); Traveller's Checklist (travel); Especially Maine (regional); The Woodworker's Store (woodworking).

How to Sell to Mail-Order Catalogs

To sell to catalogs, first research those catalogs that target the same audience as your product. If possible, get a sample copy of the catalogs and review them to see if they offer any compatible products. Then send a sample of your product to those catalogs that you think would do the best job of presenting and selling your product.

At the same time, enclose a Merchandise Data Sheet. (For a sample data sheet, see pages 163–168 of my Complete Direct Marketing Sourcebook.) This data sheet should provide all the details about your product, from its shipping weight and size to its potential markets.

To help you sell to mail-order catalog houses, here are a few magazines and directories that cover the catalog industry:

Catalog Age, Six River Bend, P.O. Box 4949, Stamford, CT 06907-0949; 203-358-9900; 800-775-3777; fax: 203-357-9014. This company also publishes Direct magazine.

DM News, 100 Avenue of the Americas, New York, NY 10013; 212-925-7300; fax: 212-925-8758. A weekly trade newspaper.

The Catalog of Catalogs, Woodbine House, 6510 Bells Mill Road, Bethesda, MD 20852; 301-897-3570; 800-843-7323. Fourteen thousand consumer catalogs arranged by subject. Cost: $24.95.

The Directory of Mail Order Catalogs, Grey House Publishing, Pocket Knife Square, P.O. Box 1866, Lakeville, CT 06069; 203-435-0868; 800-562-2139; fax: 203-435-0867. Lists seventy-three hundred mail-order catalogs. Cost: $155. This company also publishes the Directory of Business to Business Catalogs, which lists forty-three hundred business catalogs.

National Directory of Catalogs, Oxbridge Communications, 150 Fifth Ave., #303, New York, NY 10011-4311; 212-741-0231; fax: 212-633-2938. Lists nine thousand mail-order catalogs classified by subject. Cost: $345.

Catalogue of Canadian Catalogues, Alpel Publishing, P.O. Box 203, Chambly, Quebec J3L 4B3, Canada; 514-658-6205; fax: 514-658-3514; e-mail: alpelie@accent.net. Features one thousand Canadian mail-order catalogs. Cost: $16.95.

Idea 19: Publish a Mail-Order Catalog

Rather than selling to other catalogs, why not develop your own catalog? Disney has done it. Barnes & Noble has done it. Many small retailers have done it. If you don't want to start with an expensive printed catalog, start with fliers or a Web site. Build from there. Keep your catalog focused on a specific theme related to your product. Start small, with perhaps only five or ten items, and expand as the demand requires. Besides using the catalog as an additional promotion to your customers, you might also offer it to other targeted lists.

KTAV, a book publisher, started the *Jewish Gifts Catalogue*, which now includes not only books, but also cookie cutters, games, crafts, toys, and gifts. Besides being sent to individual customers, the catalog is used by

Your Customer Is Special

No matter what sort of business or service you provide, you must treat your customers right. This is especially important in mail-order and catalog businesses, where your customer is your business. John Peterman, the model for the cataloger John Peterman made famous on Seinfeld, attributes much of his success to the way he treats his customers—as he would want to be treated.

As he put it, "I think consumers are smart and have a sense of humor. We're selling individuality—life how we wish it was and how it can be. Everyone wants romance in their lives. Everyone wants to feel special."

fund-raising organizations within the Jewish community. Similarly, the Firefighter's Bookstore catalog began as a bounceback offer from Aames-Allen, the publisher of one book on home fire safety.

Idea 20: Sell Your Product As a Premium

In 1987, American businesses spent more than $23.1 billion on premiums and incentives. Of that amount, more than half was spent on incentives (20.6 percent for dealer incentives and 31.5 percent for sales incentives). Business gifts made up 12.6 percent, self-liquidators another 12.5 percent, continuity programs another 7.9 percent, and all other programs the remaining 15 percent. Ten years later, premium sales have almost doubled.

Here are just a few of the ways that companies might use your product or service as premiums or incentives:

Dealer incentives These incentives reward retailers and other dealers for displaying a manufacturer's wares prominently and/or for selling a significant amount of those wares. Most dealer incentives are for larger gifts such as trips, appliances, and gift certificates.

Sales incentives To encourage salespeople to better their previous sales records, companies often give them prizes (the greater their sales, the larger the prize). Again, most sales incentives involve higher-priced prizes such as trips or appliances.

Employee incentives These incentives are given to employees who meet certain goals (other than sales goals). For example, they might be responsible for increasing production or setting new safety records. Intracorp, a health maintenance organization (HMO), gave a copy of *Health Promotion and Medical Guide* to every one of its client's employees who chose it as their HMO. By providing this book, Intracorp hoped to decrease the number of medical claims filed by these employees and thereby cut its health-care costs. In less than two years, Intracorp gave out fifty thousand copies of the book, thus netting Random House a half-million dollars in sales.

Business gifts To show their appreciation to their major customers, businesses often give gifts during the holiday season. While in many cases, these gifts involve food for the body, there is no reason such gifts could not involve other suitable products or services. How about a massage or a beauty makeover for the holidays? Besides giving gifts to major customers, businesses also give to their employees for birthdays, weddings, illnesses, deaths, retirements, promotions, and other major events.

Company celebrations Upjohn celebrated its one hundredth anniversary by having the Benjamin Company prepare a history of its century, which it gave to its employees and customers.

Opening celebrations A Santa Barbara bank celebrated the opening of a new branch by giving away five thousand copies of Judy Dugan's self-published book *Santa Barbara Highlights and History* to every customer that came in during the first week. Home Place superstores hires Chef Harry Schwartz as the official cook for the grand openings of its stores.

Traffic builders Bamberger's department store chain gave away fifty thousand copies of *A Taste of German Cooking* (Hammond) to promote the store's restaurant during its Oktoberfest celebration.

Bonus premiums To encourage subscriptions to its magazine, *Working Woman* gave new subscribers free copies of *Boss Lady*, the autobiography of advertising executive Jo Foxworth. The response rate to the magazine's direct-mail promotions increased by 25 percent as compared to increases with other bonus giveaways they had been using.

Self-liquidators Many cereals and other food products offer special items for sale at wholesale with a small payment plus proof of purchase. Life cereal offered a Rand McNally Road Atlas for $3.50 and two UPC symbols. Grosset & Dunlap sold more than a million Nancy Drew and Hardy Boys books when they were offered as a self-liquidating premium on twenty million boxes of Post Raisin Bran cereal.

In-packs With in-packs, the premium is offered inside the package. When customers buy the product, they get the premium. Alka-Seltzer has used excerpts from several books as in-packs to promote its "relief-giving" properties. During tax time, the company gave away *Tax Relief*, an excerpt from J. K. Lasser's *Your Income Tax*.

On-packs With on-packs, the premium is offered on the outside of the package. Most on-packs are short quizzes, puzzles, or other items that can be printed on the package (like a follow-the-dots drawing on a box of cereal).

Near-packs These are premiums that are offered at the point of purchase but that are not in or attached to the product being promoted. For example, Rand McNally designed a small atlas as a near-pack to promote Cambridge cigarettes.

Selecting Premiums

HOW DO COMPANIES select premiums to use in their promotions? According to a study in Business & Incentives, here's how:

25.1% while brainstorming with management

18.7% from seeing ads in trade magazines

12.5% during trade shows

10.7% through manufacturers' representatives

 8.3% because of the popularity of past awards

 8.0% from incentive house suggestions

 7.2% by reading new product announcements in trade journals

Since trade magazines and trade shows play such an important part in the premium selection process, you should read at least one of the following magazines and attend one of the two major trade shows held every year. Besides reading the following magazines, you should also send them your publicity and test an advertisement for your premium offers.

Incentive, Bill Communications, 355 Park Ave. South, New York, NY 10010; 212-592-6400; fax: 212-592-6459. They also publish *Sales & Marketing Management*.

Potentials in Marketing, Lakewood Publications, 50 S. Ninth St., Minneapolis, MN 55402-3165; 612-333-0471; fax: 612-333-6526.

Promo, 11 Riverbend Dr. South, P.O. Box 4949, Stamford, CT 06907-0949; 203-358-9900; fax: 203-358-5834.

National Premium/Incentive Show, Hall-Erickson, 150 Burlington Ave., Clarendon Hills, IL 60514; 708-850-7779; 800-752-6312; fax: 708-850-7483. This trade show is held in Chicago in late September or early October.

Premium Incentive Show, Miller-Freeman, 1515 Broadway, New York, NY 10036; 212-626-2486; 800-950-1314; fax: 212-730-2952. This annual trade show is held in New York City in early May.

Idea 21: Use Premiums to Sell More

If you don't sell your product or service as a premium or incentive, you should still consider using premiums and

If you don't sell your product or service as a premium or incentive, you should still consider using premiums and incentives in your own business to increase orders, reward sales agents or employees, open doors, and thank referrals.

incentives in your own business to increase orders, reward sales agents or employees, open doors, thank referrals, and so on. For instance, an insurance agent could give away a tax guide to everyone who agrees to hear her sales pitch (a door opener). Or you could give away an inspirational marketing book (such as this one) each time one of your customers refers a friend to your product or service.

Idea 22: Make Other Corporate Sales

Besides premiums and sales incentives, corporations and other organizations can use other company's (like yours) products and services to their competitive advantage. Here are just a few of the other approaches you can use to sell to corporations:

Training programs Corporations and government agencies spent $60 billion in 1984 to train their employees. Why shouldn't they be using your products or services as resources in their training programs? When Roger Von Oech originally self-published *A Whack on the Side of the Head*, he sold many copies to corporations that used his book in training their creative staffs. IBM bought two thousand copies, Hewlett Packard seven hundred copies, and Control Data six hundred copies.

Health-care programs To promote the health and well-being of their employees as well as save money on health-insurance benefits, many companies have established health-care programs. To support these programs, companies often buy products or services to encourage their employees to practice healthy exercise, diet, and nutrition habits.

Retirement planning Many companies are now taking responsibility for helping their employees to make the transition to retirement. If you're a tax accountant, insurance agent, travel planner, psychologist, or career counselor, the window is wide open to help companies and their employees with health and retirement planning.

Sponsorships As part of their public relations programs, some companies will sponsor worthy causes and special projects related to those causes. If you are working with nonprofit groups, you might look to corporate sponsorships to help fund your efforts.

Bundling To add value to their product or to aid consumers in using their product, some corporations will bundle another company's product with theirs. For instance, when introducing the Laser Writer, Apple Computer included two books about the PostScript programming language along with every LaserWriter it sold.

Idea 23: Sell Sweepstakes Prizes

Any company offering a trip as a grand prize in a sweepstakes promotion could use a travel guide to the trip's destination, a camera, or special clothing as third or fourth prizes to be given away at the same time. Since sweepstakes tend to work better when there are more prizes to be awarded, such low-cost yet valuable prizes can add considerably to the perceived value of the sweepstakes.

Watch for companies that regularly run sweepstakes. In addition, look in the Resource Center in the back of each issue of *Promo* magazine for a list of those companies that set up many of the sweepstakes paid for by other companies. If your product fits in with their ongoing sweepstake offerings, contact them about using your product as one of the third or fourth prizes. Since more of the smaller prizes are given away in a sweepstakes, you are better off selling them one of these prizes than the grand prize, anyway. Still, don't expect to get paid a lot for these prizes. Discounts will be deep. But the promotional exposure alone may make it worth your while to get involved.

Idea 24: Sell Package Inserts

Include package inserts from other companies in all your outgoing mail or orders. Under this arrangement, other companies provide you with sufficient inserts and pay you $40 or more per thousand inserts. If you ship out ten thousand or more packages a year, a package insert broker could help you to locate interested companies. Here are the addresses of two well-known package insert brokers:

Leon Henry Inc., 455 Central Ave., Scarsdale,
    NY 10583; 914-723-3176; fax: 914-723-0205;
    e-mail: *lhenryinc@aol.com*; Web: *http://www.leon
    henryinc.com*.

Mokrynski Associates, 401 Hackensack Ave., Hackensack, NJ 07601; 201-488-5656; fax: 201-488-9225; e-mail: *tsulliva@mokry.attmail.com*; Web: *http://www.mokrynski.com*.

If you don't have enough outgoing packages, you might want to trade package inserts with another compatible company. You insert the other company's promotions in your outgoing orders, while that company inserts your promotions in its outgoing orders.

Idea 25: Give Your Product Away on Television Game Shows

If you want low-cost, mass exposure to a general market, look into offering your product or service as a prize in TV game shows or placing your product in a prime-time TV show or movie. One company that can help you do that is Game-Show Placements, 7011 Willoughby Ave., Hollywood, CA 90038; 213-874-7818; fax: 213-874-0643.

Reese's Pieces gained incredible sales after being featured in Steven Spielberg's classic movie *E.T: The Extra-Terrestrial.* M&Ms turned the promotion down. Too bad for them.

> If you want low-cost, mass exposure to a general market, look into offering your product or service as a prize in TV game shows or placing your product in a prime-time TV show or movie.

Idea 26: Give Your Product Away on Radio

Morning drive-time shows are always looking for products or services to give away. And they tend to have the largest audiences of any daytime show on the radio. Why not offer free dinner-for-two coupons at your restaurant? Or a free session at your marriage counseling practice? Or a free bridal bouquet? The possibilities are endless. And the exposure can be incredible.

If you have a national product, you can offer free give-aways to shows across the country. Advertising in *Radio-TV Interview Report* (see chapter 3) might be one way to make your offer known to radio producers and hosts around the country. Or you might want to try one of the following companies, which specialize in radio promotions:

Marketing Mix, 800-489-8444.

Pierce Promotions & Event Management, 4 Moulton St., Portland, ME 04101; 207-761-6504; e-mail: *promotion@maine.com*.

Today's Media Promotion Group, 106 Corporate Park Dr., White Plains, NY 10604; 914-696-0100; fax: 914-696-0119; e-mail: *JoeS@TMPG.com*.

Idea 27: Sell to Home-Shopping Networks

One way to sell a lot of products very quickly is to get your product featured on QVC or one of the other TV home-shopping networks. QVC can sell thousands of products in an hour. If you have a product with national mass-market appeal, send it directly to the home offices of the various shopping networks. If your product has a regional appeal, wait until QVC comes to your state looking for regional products to feature. Check with your state department of commerce to find out about QVC's next trip your way.

To get you started, here are the addresses of the two major home-shopping networks:

If you have a product with national mass-market appeal, send it directly to the home offices of the various shopping networks.

QVC Network, Vendor Relations Department, 1365 Enterprise Dr., Westchester, PA 19380; 610-701-8655.

Home Shopping Network, Purchasing Department, P.O. Box 9090, Clearwater, FL 34618-9090; 813-572-8585; fax: 813-573-3702.

Idea 28: Sell Your Product to an Infomercial

If you are a psychic reader, memory whiz, beauty consultant, or business success, or if you just have a unique product to sell, look into TV infomercials. Don't try to produce and market one yourself, however. Instead, look to license your product to a known producer. The landscape of producers and production companies is always changing, so we won't list them here. When you are ready to consider such a venture, contact me, John Kremer, for my $3 report *How to Sell via Television*. The report is constantly updated with the latest information. To order, contact Open Horizons, P.O. Box 205, Fairfield, IA 52556-0205; 515-472-6130; fax: 515-472-1560; e-mail: *JohnKremer@bookmarket.com*; Web: *http://www. bookmarket.com/reports.html*.

Idea 29: Syndicate Your Expertise

Once you have developed a local newspaper column or radio show, look into syndicating it nationwide. It's great

Giveaway Promotions

Proctor & Gamble starts building customer loyalty at a young age. How? By giving away school education programs tied to its products. These programs, which include teacher's guides, posters, information packets, and sample products, are provided free to any school or teacher requesting the material. Here is a sampling of their programs:

- CREST DENTAL HEALTH PROGRAM. This dental health education program for first-graders features an animated 7-minute video, a sing-along cassette, a classroom poster, and student dental health kits with samples of Crest toothpaste.

- ALWAYS CHANGING. This growth and development program for fifth-grade students features a teacher's guide with puberty/menstruation information and lesson plans, a live-action modular 28-minute video, and separate information booklets for boys and girls (with sample Always pads for the girls).

- COOL BEGINNINGS. This personal hygiene program for fifth-grade students features lesson plans, a classroom poster, and leaflets for boys (with Old Spice deodorant samples) and girls (with samples of Secret antiperspirant and Pantene shampoo).

- CLEAR CONFIDENCE. This self esteem and personal care program for seventh- grade students features a 16-minute video, 10 Steps to Self Esteem posters, and product samples of Clearasil, Pert Plus, and Sure.

publicity for your company or service. Here are some syndication success stories:

Syndicated newspaper columns Mary Ellen Pinkham, author of a number of books on helpful hints, writes a syndicated column that is carried by more than 125 newspapers with a combined circulation of well over ten million readers.

Several parenting columns written by relationship counselors are also syndicated nationally.

Television features After publishing her books on helpful hints, Pinkham joined *Good Morning America* for two years as a commentator on helpful hints for the home. Similarly, chef Harry Schwartz is a regular guest on NBC's *Today* program.

Syndicated television show Howard Ruff, author of *How to Prosper during the Coming Bad Years*, had a nationally syndicated TV show called *Ruff Times.*

Syndicated radio series Beverly Nye, self-publisher of *A Family Raised on Sunshine*, syndicated her own series of shows on homemaking tips to radio stations across the country. Not only did the radio stations pay her royalties for airing the show, but she was able to use the show to plug her books.

Magazine columnist Herschell Gordon Lewis, author of *Direct Mail Copy That Sells*, writes a regular column for *Direct* magazine. At the end of each column, the magazine prints a short biography that plugs his copywriting services.

Newsletter columnist Before getting his regular magazine column, Lewis wrote a copywriting column for a direct-marketing newsletter.

Idea 30: Become a Consultant

If you are not comfortable speaking before large groups or committing to writing regular columns, you can still put

If you are not comfortable speaking before large groups or committing to writing regular columns, you can still put your expertise to work as a consultant.

your expertise to work as a consultant. No matter what your subject area, somewhere at sometime someone will need your expertise—and be willing to pay well for your services. In the meantime, your consulting work helps to promote your other services or products.

To learn more about setting yourself up as a consultant, read Jeffrey Lant's *The Consultant's Kit*, Herman Holtz's *How to Succeed As an Independent Consultant*, or Kate Kelly's *How to Set Your Fees and Get Them*. All three books are superb. You might also want to subscribe to *Consulting Opportunities Journal*, P.O. Box 430, Clear Spring, MD 21722; 301-791-9332.

Here are a few ways to conduct your consulting services:

Offer onsite consulting services Besides producing about fifty seminars every year on construction estimating and project management, the R. S. Means Company also publishes software and offers consulting services where they send experts to work with construction companies onsite.

Offer consulting services via mail Herschell Gordon Lewis, author of a number of books on direct marketing, has his own business called Communicomp, which offers direct-mail copywriting for a wide variety of companies and organizations including the UN Children's Fund, Grolier Enterprises, Heritage House, and American Bankers Insurance Company. All his business is conducted through the mail and by phone.

Offer telephone consulting As the author of a number of books on book marketing and editor of

Book Marketing Update, I also offer telephone consulting to anyone who has questions about book publishing and marketing. I charge $120 per hour or $2 per minute for this service. I do little promotion for this service and do not actively solicit consulting work, but I still end up consulting about five to ten hours per month for an income of $600 to $1,200 per month from consulting. And the consulting invariably leads to additional book and database sales.

Franchise your consulting services Carole Jackson, author of the multimillion-copy bestseller *Color Me Beautiful*, has franchised Color Me Beautiful consultants all over the country. When Acropolis Books came out with a new book, *Always in Style with Color Me Beautiful* by Doris Pooser, its thirty-city publicity campaign was fully supported by Color Me Beautiful consultants in each of those cities.

Idea 31: Organize Your Own Seminars

Seminars and workshops are a great way to promote your expertise, and promoting your expertise is the best way to convince people to buy your products or services. A gourmet shop can offer cooking classes. A beauty shop can offer hair care seminars. A psychologist can offer marriage workshops. The list is endless. No matter what your product or service, you should be able to develop and promote a workshop that will draw upon and highlight your expertise.

Seminars and workshops are a great way to promote your expertise, and promoting your expertise is the best way to convince people to buy your products or services.

Once you've had some experience as a speaker and consultant, you might consider setting up seminars like the "Implementing in Search of Excellence" seminars (informally known as skunkcamps) put on by Tom Peters. The skunkcamps are only one of five services offered by the Tom Peters Group; the other four are consulting, research, publishing, and audio/video products.

Gordon Burgett conducts hundreds of seminars every year. All of his seminars and books cover the same subjects: freelance writing, travel writing, making money as a speaker, and giving seminars. His speaking seminar is now available as a course on cassette tape. For more information, write to Communication Unlimited, P.O. Box 6405, Santa Maria, CA 93456; 805-937-8711; fax: 805-937-3035.

Idea 32: Get Your Message Out—Uniquely

Here are a few offbeat ways to get your message out to more people:

Inserts in shopping bags Some paper bag companies are now offering to insert advertising messages inside shopping bags at a relatively low cost per thousand.

Printed bags, cartons, and matchbooks Market-test having your advertising message printed on the outside of grocery bags and other shopping bags where people besides the recipient will see your ad. Some producers of milk cartons are also offering to print appropriate advertising messages on the outside of their cartons. And, of course, there are always matchbooks, a longtime advertising vehicle for correspondence courses.

Ad specialties and premiums Print your promotional message on anything from a mousepad to a baseball cap, from a slide chart to a coffee mug. Try to match the premium or advertising specialty to your product or service. Please don't send any more pens. But how about stickers, decals, buttons, balloons, memo cubes, notepads, rubber stamps, golf balls, calculators, oversize paper clips, rulers, playing cards, yo-yos, thermometers, magnetic message holders, wine glasses, pot holders, key chains, or ice scrapers? If you're a marriage coach, how about baseball caps? If a diet counselor, how about a calorie-counter slide chart? If a budget counselor, how about a coupon clipper? For more information about ad specialties, send for a free booklet, *Specialty Advertising: The Medium That Remains to Be Seen.* Write to the Promotional Products Association International, 3125 Skyway Circle North, Irving, TX 75038-3526; 214-252-0404; fax: 214-594-7224.

T-shirts and other apparel T-shirts are walking billboards. If you can convince people to wear your T-shirts (especially retailers), then you'll have a much better chance of getting your product noticed. How about sun visors for a golf product, muscle T-shirts for a health club, or bikinis for a diet service? One way to distribute imprinted apparel is to offer a free T-shirt with every order of ten or more items. Or give items away to a sampling of people at a public event (for example, imprinted baseball caps at a baseball game). Or give them to people who will wear them on crowded streets during lunch hour.

Calendars Calendars can be a superb way to advertise a product or service. That's why banks give them away. But why not a pizza parlor? If you decide to create promotional calendars, do not send generic calendars imprinted with your company name. Use photos or illustrations that truly relate to your product or service.

One way to distribute imprinted apparel is to offer a free T-shirt with every order of ten or more items.

Idea 33: Distribute Your Fliers

If you have a local product or service, print up some inexpensive fliers and have them distributed in the local area by neighborhood kids or by a professional distribution service. Start by testing a small area and see if you get any results (sales!). If you do get results and the sales are enough to cover your expenses, distribute some more fliers over a wider area.

Look for the right places to distribute your fliers. For example, if you have an automotive service or product, distribute fliers under the windshield wipers of targeted cars at shopping centers, in downtown parking lots, or at the beach.

Idea 34: Hang Posters

Why not poster the town? If it works for garage sales and circuses, why not for your business? Whenever we visit New York, we always see thousands of posters decorating construction sites announcing new plays or movies. Why couldn't another product or service be publicized in the same way?

Idea 35: Give Out Samples

Another ubiquitous phenomenon we've noticed on New York streets is the people giving away samples (cigarettes, candy, and more). Again, why not give away samples of your product? You could also distribute samples through participating retailers, exhibits, conferences, meetings, and other group events or public areas. Distribute samples anywhere there are plenty of people who might be interested in your product. Day-Timer, through fifteen trained counselors, has distributed more than 750,000 samples of its products in one year. The company has found sampling to be the best method to introduce its organizers to new audiences.

If your product or service has a targeted audience, send samples or brochures to opinion leaders. When Warner Books published John Naisbitt's *Megatrends*, it sent sample copies to the chief executives of the five hundred largest corporations in the country. As a result, the publisher "created a groundswell of acknowledgment" for the book.

If your product or service has a targeted audience, send samples or brochures to opinion leaders.

Idea 36: Advertise in Public Places

Here are some of the many public places where you can advertise. In some cases, you can advertise quite cheaply.

Stadium advertising If you have a product or service that appeals to sports audiences, try stadium advertising. You don't have to limit such advertising to baseball or football stadiums. You could also use basketball arenas, boxing gyms, dance halls, or convention centers—wherever an audience interested in your product or service might gather.

Blimps, balloons, and airplanes Goodyear is probably better known for its blimp than for any other advertising it does. Currently a number of other companies are flying blimps as well as hot air balloons and airplanes to publicize their company name at public events. Skywriting and banners flown from an airplane could work well to promote a single event.

Billboards Billboards can be effective as reminder advertising to reinforce other forms of advertising or promotion. Bantam Doubleday Dell, for example, has used billboards combined with national advertising and an author tour to promote Joseph Heller's novel *God Knows*. Of course, a single billboard could be your sole advertising vehicle. One aspiring actress has had a billboard on Sunset Boulevard in Hollywood for years—and she has received lots of press attention.

Display billboards in malls Many shopping malls and airport terminals now offer space on their walls for billboard advertising. Day-Timer has found that its billboard advertising in airport terminals has yielded thousands of inquiries and orders every week for its organizers.

Transit advertising Over the years, the sides and interior of buses, subways, bus stops, and taxis have been used to advertise countless products and ser-

Traveling Billboards

The possibilities for traveling billboards are endless. Here are just a few recent innovations in transit advertising:

➡ During the mad cow scare in England, one enterprising farmer near Birmingham, England, decided to increase his revenue by selling advertising space on the sides of his cows. He charges $450 per week for the cow placards. As he noted, "The cows are losing money while they are feeding [since they cannot be sold], so they might as well start paying for their upkeep." He sold eight such ads.

➡ A local sign shop in Miami, Florida, provides panhandlers with professionally made signs pleading for handouts. In addition, the signs include an advertisement for the sign shop. The owner then pays the panhandlers a percentage of any business they generate.

➡ Mike Cutino, publisher of New York Sports Scene magazine, claims that 75 percent of his 125,000 circulation has come from billboards on trucks. In fact, he likes the billboard trucks so much that he bought the company.

vices. If you advertise your products or services through transit ads, try to include a "Take One" order pad attached to the ad so that interested commuters can easily respond. One advantage of transit ads over billboards is that the transit ad travels all over the city.

Delivery trucks Several services (such as Advan out of San Francisco and Wheeler Inc. out of Long Island) offer moving ads on delivery trucks. How much does it cost to place such an ad? About $9,000 per month. Advan claims to deliver thirty-three thousand impressions a day—which reportedly are quite effective in building a company's image.

Other billboard ads A few other billboard-type ads that have been used include bench ads (at bus stops or in parks), sandwich boards circulated in heavy pedestrian traffic, picket advertising, parking meter ads, shopping carts, ski lifts, bumper stickers, and "Johnny ads" (yep, you guessed it, these are ads in public toilet facilities).

Idea 37: Give Out Business Cards

Think of your business cards as wallet-sized billboards, and use them accordingly. Business cards can be one of your most effective promotional tools, especially as facilitators of networking opportunities.

Flash Your Business Card

Business cards work a whole lot harder these days. No longer a bland black and white, business cards now come in all colors, from hot pink to fluorescent orange, with color photographs, intricate illustrations, cutouts, pop-ups, or holograms. And business cards no longer come only in plain paper, but in all sorts of materials, from magnetic cards to wood, leather, fluorescent plastic, translucent cellulose, and heat sensitive materials. In keeping with the digital age, you can now send a virtual business card via e-mail.

But don't treat business cards as attention-getters only; they can also do a selling job for your product or service. For instance, George Allen of GFA Management, a real estate investment firm, hands out a one-fold business card that features a loan amortization chart as well as an income capitalization valuation formula. Ogden, Utah, real estate agent Ron McCall passes out a business card that features a list of local retailers and restaurants on the back. All of those listed on the back offer special discounts to anyone presenting Ron's business card.

Idea 38: Advertise in Movie Theaters

Theaters have begun interspersing commercials with movie previews before the feature film. I've seen ads for Wrangler jeans, General Electric radios, and O'Dell's butter (besides, of course, the popcorn and candy commercials produced by Coke, Pepsi, or 7-Up). How effective are such pre-movie commercials? While the same number of people will see a commercial in movie theaters during one month (if the commerical has national coverage) as will see an average commercial on television (about thirty million), one study reports that more than four times as many people will remember the movie commercial the day after as will remember the TV commercial.

Idea 39: Advertise in the Yellow Pages

People rarely look at the yellow pages unless they are actively pursuing the purchase of a product or hiring of a service. Advertising in the yellow pages is one of the lowest-cost, highest-impact promotions you can do. Almost 80 percent (76.7 to be exact) of all adults refer to the yellow pages in a typical month. On a typical day, the yellow pages are referred to forty-nine million times. Half of all yellow pages references result in the purchase of a product or service.

There are more than sixty-four hundred yellow pages directories published in the United States. Many of these directories offer per inquiry advertising deals or split runs to encourage national advertisers to run an ad. Indeed, you need not limit your advertising to the local directory. It is possible to buy space through a national network of yellow pages if you have a product or service that would interest a specific national audience. One food company is advertising cents-off coupons for their frozen pizzas under the Pizza listing in local phone books.

Half of all yellow pages references result in the purchase of a product or service.

Idea 40: Place an In-Store Advertisement

Some grocery stores and shopping malls now provide their own in-store background music programming. Often they also sell advertising on these broadcasts. Campbell Soup has used such in-store ads to build consumer interest in their Le Menu frozen dinners. Two major advantages of such advertising: It reaches buyers when they are in a buying mood and where the product is readily available for purchase.

Idea 41: Explore Multilevel Marketing

Multilevel marketing (sometimes also known as network marketing) has successfully launched many new products, including Amway, Shaklee, blue-green algae, vitamins, beauty products, and much more. It's especially useful for promoting products that need to be explained to be appreciated. If you are interested in this means of marketing, check it out carefully beforehand. Many network marketing plans are little more than pyramid schemes, which draw governmental scrutiny. Also be cautious in using this means for marketing your product, because it is still associated in many minds with fly-by-night operators and zealous proselytizers. Multilevel marketing hasn't yet taken advantage of its full potential. Perhaps someday someone will come up with a way to draw upon the strengths of multilevel marketing without incorporating its weaknesses.

If you are interested in multilevel marketing, check it out carefully beforehand. Many network marketing plans are little more than pyramid schemes, which draw governmental scrutiny.

Idea 42: Run a Sweepstakes

In a poll conducted by *Premium/Incentive Business*, more than 96 percent of the companies that ran sweepstakes accomplished their goals. For these companies, sweep-stakes helped to increase sales, public awareness, brand recognition, and/or store traffic. Sweepstakes have also been known to boost response to direct-mail promotions by as much as 50 percent.

If you decide to run a sweepstakes, you should hire a company that specializes in managing sweepstakes and other contests. The legal requirements for sweepstakes are so exacting that you shouldn't even try to offer one without advice from an experienced consultant. Besides helping you to meet the legal requirements, these companies can provide creative development, prize selection and acquisition, judges, and fulfillment. Their services are well worth any additional cost. For more information, write or call one of the following companies, which specialize in sweepstakes, contests, and other promotions:

Don Jagoda Associates, 100 Marcus Dr., Melville, NY 11747; 516-454-1800; fax: 516-454-1833; e-mail: *info@dja.com.*

FAC Services Group, 111 E. Wacker Dr., Chicago, IL 60601; 312-938-341; fax: 312-938-2296.

Marden-Kane Inc., 36 Maple Place, Manhasset, NY 11030-1962; 516-365-3999; fax: 516-365-5250; 312-266-4919 (Chicago); 818-905-6301 (Los Angeles).

PMC Partnership Ltd., 19 Ludlow Road, #302, Westport, CT 06880; 203-227-8478.

The Sweepstakes Center, 2290 East Ave., Rochester, NY 14610; 716-256-0080; e-mail: *sweepnet@ ice-net.com.* Custom or shared sweepstakes from

The legal requirements for sweepstakes are so exacting that you shouldn't even try to offer one without advice from an experienced consultant.

concept through fulfillment. Call for the free '97
Sweepstakes Guide and sample kit.

Ventura Associates, 1040 Avenue of the Americas,
New York, NY 10018; 212-302-8277; fax: 212-
302-2587.

Idea 43: Run a Contest

Another way to generate interest is to sponsor contests
that are in some way connected to your product or service. Unlike sweepstakes, contests can be tests of knowledge, skill, or some other capability.

In the back of book #12 in its Sweet Valley High series,
Bantam printed two dozen questions based on the first
twelve books of the series. Bantam received more than
twenty thousand entries. Winners were randomly chosen
from those who answered all the questions correctly. The
prizes included a trip to New York City to meet Francine
Pascal, creator of the series, as well as tickets to a
Broadway show and a visit to the set of *All My Children*.
The contest had its desired effect. Sales of backlist titles
increased considerably. As an added benefit, Bantam was
able to develop a list of teenage romance readers. Since the
contest, Bantam has sent these readers newsletters and announcements about new series that might interest them.

Unlike sweepstakes, contests can be tests of knowledge, skill, or some other capability.

Idea 44: Brandstand Your Product

"Brandstanding" is the linking of special events with specific brands or products. For instance, Budweiser and

Pepsi sponsor a number of different sports events each year. Miller sponsors golf games. Virginia Slims sponsors tennis tournaments. Why couldn't a health club, health food store, or diet coach help to sponsor a run-for-fun event?

Idea 45: Use Alternative Media

Besides statement stuffers and card packs, there are now a good number of other alternative media (ridealongs or piggybacks) that may be effective for marketing your products or services. With the high cost of postage, these alternative media are making more and more sense, especially if you want to reach a mass audience.

What are some of the advantages of piggybacking your advertising message with someone else's?

1. Your offer receives an implied endorsement from the company sponsoring the alternative medium.

2. The cost is 75 to 80 percent less than a solo mailing.

3. With more than two thousand piggyback programs available, it's possible to target almost any mass audience.

For more details about these alternative media (including a checklist of their pitfalls), send for a copy of *Alternative Media: The Time Has Finally Come!* This special report is available free to direct marketers who contact Leon Henry Inc., 455 Central Ave., Scarsdale, NY

10583; 914-723-3176; fax: 914-723-0205. Leon Henry is a leading supplier of alternative media programs.

The following pages describe a few of the alternative media you could use to promote your products:

Package insert programs Earlier we suggested that you offer other companies opportunities in your order fulfillment. Advertising inserts are sent along with merchandise shipments from catalogs and other direct marketers such as Spiegel, Book-of-the-Month Club, Hanover House, Fingerhut, Field Publications, McCalls Cooking School, and Lillian Vernon. Besides the strong implied endorsement, package insert programs allow you to reach hotline buyers.

Statement stuffers These are advertising inserts that ride along with customer invoices, statements, and renewal efforts from banks, magazines, credit card issuers, cable services, phone companies, utilities, and other monthly billers. They allow you to reach credit-worthy customers at a low cost. One disadvantage, however, is that statements are a negative buying environment (the recipients are being reminded of a debt).

Ridealong programs Your advertising message is inserted into other direct marketers' prospecting programs. Besides allowing package inserts in their outgoing merchandise shipments, Columbia House, Doubleday Book Clubs, and BMG Music also sometimes include other companies' advertising messages in their promotional mailings.

Similarly, some catalogs feature bound-in post-cards or other inserts advertising compatible products. Gardener's Choice, Gurney Seed, and Gander Mountain are among the catalogs that offer this choice.

Card decks There are more than seven hundred card decks reaching targeted audiences, from doctors and dentists to sales executives and computer professionals. It is best to use these card packs to generate leads and sell high-priced products or services.

National co-op mailings These co-op programs, which reach large audiences (rarely less than a million), feature a mix of coupons and direct-response inserts. Such programs are usually packaged in 6 × 9-inch full-color envelopes. For example, Larry Tucker's co-op marketing programs reach 4 million college students, 7 million elementary students, 4 million high school students, 10 million older people, 3.5 million new parents, and 6.5 million parents of preschoolers once or twice a year. For a list of such programs, check out the resources section in *Promo* magazine.

Catalog request services Your catalog could be featured in the many new catalog request services such as that provided by Nationwide Shopper Systems. These mailings allow consumers to request catalogs that interest them. Some of these services charge a small fee per catalog ($1 to $3), while some offer catalogs free and add a small handling fee of $5 or less.

Coupon booklets You could offer a cents-off coupon for your product or service. Many coupon booklets are developed by local fund-raisers. Nationally, Home Coupon Direct mails forty million coupon books five times a year to consumers across the country.

"Take one" displays Your inserts or brochures are placed on racks in high-visibility locations. Programs reach families (Good Neighbor), college students (College Take-Ones), travelers (Tourist Take Ones), and golfers (MarketSource).

Newspaper FSIs These full-color free-standing inserts (FSIs) feature display ads, coupons, and direct-response offers in Sunday newspapers. Most are for mass-market audiences. Remnant space in FSIs can be had for as little as $1.90 to $5.75 per thousand. Costs include printing and distribution. Two companies that publish these FSIs: Quad Marketing, News America FSI, 1290 Avenue of the Americas, New York, NY 10104; 212-603-6000; 800-462-0852. Valassis Inserts, 36111 Schoolcroft Road, Livonia, MI 48150; 313-591-3000; 800-437-0479.

Idea 46: Offer a Free Lunch

Get customers to come to you by offering an unrelated benefit. For instance, one plumbing store offered free coffee and hot dogs for lunch every day. Plumbers stopped by

> **Get customers to come to you by offering an unrelated benefit. For instance, one plumbing store offered free coffee and hot dogs for lunch every day.**

for the free lunch and stayed to buy things they needed. Why limit such offerings to open houses or opening-day activities? Use them all month long. Be sure, however, to check local health regulations before offering this enticement.

Idea 47: Do Everything

If you have the time, you can be your own best salesperson. Sharon Scott is responsible for selling thousands of copies of her two books, *Peer Pressure Reversal* and *How to Say No and Keep Your Friends.* We list just a few of the activities that have helped to sell her books. You should be able to do as much or more for your product or service.

➡ She conducts in-service training programs for teachers, counselors, and parents.

➡ Through seminars and workshops, she has trained twenty-five hundred students.

➡ She speaks at many conferences, both regional and national, for professionals working with youth.

➡ She writes a "Positive Parenting" column that appears in many school newsletters.

➡ She is a frequent guest on local and national TV and radio shows.

➡ She is now producing several videos based on her work.

Idea 48: Do It Once, Sell It Forever

When John Shuttleworth started *Mother Earth News* magazine, his guiding principle was this: Do it once, sell it forever. And that's just what he did. Not only did he write and edit the bimonthly magazine, but he also wrote a syndicated newspaper column three times a week, hosted a spot radio program five times a week, wrote several books, conducted dozens of seminars, and ran a mail-order business.

How did he do all this? By doing something once and then selling it over and over again. He'd write a magazine article and then whittle it down to three or four key paragraphs for the newspaper column. He'd then take the newspaper column, make a few minor changes in it, and use it as the script for his radio spots. One of the books he wrote was essentially a collection of his newspaper columns. And all the material was used as background for his seminars.

There's no reason you can't do the same when promoting your product or service. Just follow John's golden rule: Do it once, sell it forever. Have fun!

When John Shuttleworth started Mother Earth News magazine, his guiding principle was this: Do it once, sell it forever.

Index

Small Business Toolkit—
Marketing for the Self-Employed

Martin Edic

U.S. $15.00
Can. $19.95
ISBN 0-7615-0592-X
paperback / 368 pages

If you can reach the people who want to buy your products or services, you can ensure your success. That's marketing. Yet many self-employed people never master the art. You'll learn how to do it here from someone who's done it himself—profitably. Topics include:

• Effective marketing: Using your own goals and the true nature of your product or service to discover your best markets.

• Tools and tactics: Putting that all-important personal touch in all your advertising, publicity, networking, and personal sales.

• Time and money management: Maximizing these crucial ingredients of every marketing plan.

Visit us online at www.primapublishing.com

Small Business Toolkit—
Sales for the Self-Employed

Martin Edic

U.S. $15.00
Can. $19.95
ISBN 0-7615-0593-8
paperback / 336 pages

Sales—they're the measure of success. There's always another sales pitch you can make, one that succeeds where others have failed. In the same way, there's always something new to learn about how to sell effectively.

Marketing consultant and small-business owner Martin Edic shares the secrets of effective sales that he's learned in over 16 years of entrepreneurial success. He teaches you how to:

- Prospect for customers
- Assess their needs and ability to buy
- Present your product to them
- Seal the deal
- Make fear and rejection work for you
- And much more!

Visit us online at www.primapublishing.com

To Order Books

Please send me the following items:

Quantity	Title	Unit Price	Total
_____	Sales for the Self-Employed	$ 15.00	$ _____
_____	Marketing for the Self-Employed	$ 15.00	$ _____
_____	_____	$ _____	$ _____
_____	_____	$ _____	$ _____
_____	_____	$ _____	$ _____

Subtotal	$ _____
Deduct 10% when ordering 3-5 books	$ _____
7.25% Sales Tax (CA only)	$ _____
8.25% Sales Tax (TN only)	$ _____
5.0% Sales Tax (MD and IN only)	$ _____
7.0% G.S.T. Tax (Canada only)	$ _____
Shipping and Handling*	$ _____
Total Order	$ _____

*Shipping and Handling depend on Subtotal.

Subtotal	Shipping/Handling
$0.00–$14.99	$3.00
$15.00–$29.99	$4.00
$30.00–$49.99	$6.00
$50.00–$99.99	$10.00
$100.00–$199.99	$13.50
$200.00+	Call for Quote

Foreign and all Priority Request orders:
Call Order Entry department
for price quote at 916-632-4400

This chart represents the total retail price of books only
(before applicable discounts are taken).

By Telephone: With MC or Visa, call 800-632-8676 or 916-632-4400. Mon–Fri, 8:30-4:30.

WWW: http://www.primapublishing.com

By Internet E-mail: sales@primapub.com

By Mail: Just fill out the information below and send with your remittance to:

**Prima Publishing
P.O. Box 1260BK
Rocklin, CA 95677**

My name is _____

I live at _____

City _____ State _____ ZIP _____

MC/Visa# _____ Exp. _____

Check/money order enclosed for $ _____ Payable to Prima Publishing

Daytime telephone _____

Signature _____